Calm and Clear

Lama Mipham

Calm and Clear

Mi-pham 'Jam-dbyangs rnam-gyal rgya-mtsho

The Wheel of Analytic Meditation
*Sems-kyi dpyod-pa rnam-par sbyong-ba so-sor brtag-pa'i
dpyad sgom 'khor-lo-ma zhes bya-ba bzhugs-so*

Instructions on Vision in the Middle Way
Dbu-ma'i lta khrid zab-mo bzhugs-so

Translated from the Tibetan with commentary by
Tarthang Tulku

Foreword by Herbert V. Guenther

DHARMA PUBLISHING

Tibetan Translation Series

Calm and Clear
The Legend of the Great Stupa
Mind in Buddhist Psychology
Golden Zephyr
Kindly Bent to Ease Us

International Standard Book Number: 0-913546-02-x
Library of Congress Catalog Card Number: 73-79058

Typeset in Fototronic Times Roman and printed by
Dharma Press, Emeryville, California
9 8 7 6 5 4

*May these texts help people to help themselves,
That all striving be for the liberation
of all beings!*

Acknowledgements

The translation and commentary found herein were edited by Keith Dowman in the spring of 1972. A previous edition of the same material prepared by Mervin V. Hanson during the winter and spring of 1971 was consulted for this work. Mention must also be made of John Reynolds, who was the first person to work on the translation of these texts with Tarthang Tulku.

We wish to also extend our appreciation to Arthur Okamura for the cover design and the illustrations found herein and to Glen Eddy for his frontispiece drawing of Lama Mipham.

Foreword

Tarthang Tulku and I met in India more than a decade ago. At that time I was in charge of the Department of Buddhist Philosophy and Tibetan Studies at the Sanskrit University in Varanasi. The Indian government had made available fellowships for learned Lamas and scholarships for promising Tibetan students, and had entrusted me with the development of a program that was not only new then but is still without parallel in the field of Tibetan studies. The belief, still widely held both in India and the Western world, that the Tibetan tradition of Buddhism was hardly anything more than a repository of lost Sanskrit works, suffered a severe blow with the arrival of the Tibetans and the texts they brought along. It is true that many texts had been translated from Sanskrit and Prakrit into Tibetan, but it is also a fact that the compilers of these translations into the well-known collections of the bKa'-'gyur and bsTan-'gyur, excluded an unspecified number of works which belonged to an earlier tradition that did not emphasize the later Indian preference for epistemological questions. Actually, the early history of Buddhism in Tibet is still shrouded in darkness. The official version is so politically tainted that it is far from reliable. At the present stage of our knowledge we can only say that a distinction must be made between a tradition that is based on the translation from Sanskrit works that were alleged to have been composed by Indians and hence considered to be authentic and authoritative, and a tradition that long before this eclectic trend had been inspired by Buddhists who were not necessarily Indians. When in defence of this older tradition it is claimed that the texts belonging to this period present the spirit of Buddhism rather than its mere letter as contained in the so-called 'New Tradition', an important observation has been made. We, too, distinguish between the 'living spirit' of a movement and its 'dead letter'. Applied to the Buddhism of Tibet, the term 'living spirit' indicates that the tradition which is based upon it, i.e., the 'Old Tradition' (*rnying-ma*), came into existence during the formative period of Buddhism in Central Asia. It is quite likely that at that time the Tibetans contributed as much as they received. To trace the history of ideas will be the task of the future and it will be quite different from any political history which is conspicuous by the absence of any ideas at all.

Tarthang Tulku belongs to the 'Old Tradition', and when we met I had been looking for a representative of this tradition, who would be willing to share his knowledge with those eager to learn more rather than to be content with the few crumbs available. And so, when Tarthang Tulku on my recommendation became a fellow at the Sanskrit University, a time of a most prosperous co-operation ensued, for Tarthang Tulku was eager to have his tradition known and kept alive, while I was interested in what the 'living spirit' of Buddhism might have to say to modern man. I did not believe that anything had been said when, as is still customary among many academic circles, it is for instance stated that the Tibetan word *stong-pa-nyid* is the translation of the Sanskrit word *śūnyatā* and when the person to whom this profound statement is addressed is not told what those persons who used either word wanted to convey to their listeners. So Tarthang Tulku and I sat together, checking each interpretation of ideas against their textual background in the light of the use of these terms within a given context. For, let it be said quite plainly, we do not understand words and, even less so, ideas by their etymology or their origin, but by the way in which the speaker uses them.

In the history of Buddhist thought meditation has always played a major role. As we usually understand this term, it implies a definite directing or focusing of thought and, in particular, it suggests an effort to understand the thing so considered in all its aspects, relationships, and values. It is not necessarily an effort to work out a definite problem. In its religious context meditation is claimed to be an enhancement of life's powerfulness, and in order to achieve the latter, attempts are made to suppress consciousness completely, whether by drugs of various kinds, asceticism or other means which are often indistinguishable from, if not identical with, mental derangement. Common to all such attempts is the pervasive feeling of the importance of oneself, be this self-importance a plain case of megalomania—'the world could not do without me'—or an instance of self-debasement—'I am just a chattel of some transcendental hocus-pocus'. In either case a fiction is allowed to dominate and, as the Buddhist texts repeatedly assert, it does not matter whether one is fettered by a rope of straw or a chain of gold. The fact remains that we are fettered, in bondage, and are not really ourselves. The fiction of a self or *the* Self is a postulate elevated into a metaphysical principle; it has, and here again the Buddhist texts are quite explicit, its root in 'ignorance', the inability (and maybe also the unwillingness) to acknowledge the fact that the word 'I' is merely a noise coming from a speaker and does not stand for any thing or person as does, for instance, the word 'table'. Buddhist meditation is not concerned with a self, be this a super-self or a transcendental self or any other fiction, but rather with breaking through the stranglehold of this fiction and letting man's real identity emerge. Meditation thus aims at an identity experience of which any form of a self-image is but a distortion and a travesty. It is the nature of every self-image that it can see the world only as an extension of this image. If a man is a football player he plays to prove his ability, to impress others, and to make money; if he believes himself to be a great lover and makes love to a woman he does so to prove his virility. Such a person merely vegetates in a world of concepts, abstractions, beliefs and stereotypes which have little to do with the real world. Such a man, in other words, has no depths, no real being; he is merely a surface phenomenon floating from one fiction to another and producing all the time new fictions that are as irrelevant as the old ones.

Man experiences the reality of the world through his body in the sense that the body is the focal point through which he responds to the impressions he receives and on account of which there is for him a world. The manner in which he conceives of his body may facilitate or impede his activity. Usually, man tends to overestimate or underevaluate his body. The analysis of the body, with which according to the text translated here, meditation begins, is not meant to disparage the body but to bring it into proper perspective. By understanding the body as an image or a set of images we free ourselves from the dominance of these images. In a certain sense, then, the body is and is not. It is insofar as it is more responsive and it is not insofar as it is no longer a postulate demanded within the frame-work of a theory about it. The more alive the body is and the less it is a 'dead' thing, the more vividly can man perceive and appreciate reality as it is and respond to it naturally without preconceptions. Therefore, what at first appears as a denigration is a very effective means of breaking the obsession with the body as something that can and must be manipulated for selfish purposes, and it is by breaking this fixational obsession that we learn to see with an immediacy which lets things appear in a magic glow, as it were, without detracting from their intrinsic value of being.

The same analysis has to be applied to what is called 'mind'. Most of our experiences are filtered through a system of categories, constructs, fictions, and rubrics, always ego-centred on the assumption that the world can be seen only from the vantage point of the interests or demands of the perceiver. Such demanding perception actually distorts whatever is so perceived; it is always an attempt to force things to be what they never can be and the self-defeating struggle against a natural response to things by just letting them be. Letting things be is another way of getting things into proper perspective. As contrasted with the previous preoccupation with the fictions of one's own making and imposing them on what there is, it seems as if mind has become 'empty'. It is unfortunate that our language has to use this misleading term for an original term that has nothing in it of this negativism. What has happened is not that mind is lost in a bleak desert or in desolate wastelands in which there is literally nothing, but that it has been enriched beyond measure and that this richness defies any comparison with the paltry contents of ordinary perception. In the same way as the body is not denied or despised by contrasting it with an allegedly superior mind, so also mind is not suppressed for the sake of a hysterically advertised 'spirituality'. What we call 'body' and 'mind' are mere abstractions from an identity experience that cannot be reduced to the one or the other abstraction, nor can it be hypostatized into some sort of thing without falsifying its very being. Thus Buddhist meditation differs from other forms by helping man to be, rather than to subordinate him to something or other or to wipe him out by demanding the impossible. By restoring man's being it is therapeutical in the best sense of the word.

The text which Tarthang Tulku together with his disciples has translated here under the title *Calm and Clear,* has as its author the famous Mi-pham 'Jam-dbyangs rnam-rgyal rgya-mtsho (1846-1914), who is counted among the gTer-ston, teachers of the 'Concealed Teachings' (*gter-ma*). By this term reference is made to the fact that the texts of the 'Old Tradition' which did not tally with the formalized Buddhism that was vigorously propagated by the Indians coming to Tibet, were hidden at the times of the kings Khri-srong bde-btsan (755-787) and gLang-dar-ma (836-842). Later on these 'concealed teachings' were attributed to Padma Sambhava and by this association became acceptable to the partisans of the Indian faction of Buddhism. Furthermore, it was stated that they would be 'rediscovered' in the future. We can easily see that these texts are not so much works that have been literally concealed and then again unearthed, but that they continue to present the 'living spirit' of Buddhism. As a matter of fact, ideas have their roots in the past ('concealed') but bear fruit 'in the future', because it is in the light of our present experience ('discovering') that we project our future attitudes, the action of this projection taking place here and now.

It is my sincere hope that Tarthang Tulku's work—he himself belongs to the line of gTer-ston, drawing on the past but looking forward—will prosper and help those who are seekers.

HERBERT V. GUENTHER

University of Saskatchewan
Saskatoon, Sask.
Canada

Contents

PART ONE: THE WHEEL OF
ANALYTIC MEDITATION

Introduction   29
Root Verses   43
Commentary   55

PART TWO: INSTRUCTIONS ON VISION
IN THE MIDDLE WAY

Introduction   97
Root Verses - Commentary   101

Tibetan Texts   113

Selected Readings   123

Index   125

Preface

The translations of these short texts have taken many turns and, ultimately, over three years of effort. They are a consequence of Tarthang Tulku's teaching in Berkeley, and reflect his ongoing search for methods and concepts which make the depth and subtlety of Buddhism available to the modern West. Concern for presenting Buddhism in forms which both accurately represent its theory and inspire its practice has been the main reason for our selecting these two texts from among the thousands of profound volumes found in the Nyingma literature.

Both texts are short, relatively simple, practice-oriented, and emphasize a step-by-step development which begins at the most fundamental level. Thus they encourage people to begin while discouraging inappropriate beginnings and false efforts. Although we may feel that we understand such basic themes as 'impermanence' and 'unsatisfactoriness', and have dwelt on the (imagined) beauties of enlightenment, actually, meditative realization has little to do with what we *think* we know or with what we *prefer*. The conditioned nature of all existence, including the un-stable and limiting structures which we take to be our 'selves', the attachment and consequent misery which result from this pandering to the 'ego', all must be carefully attended to and understood within the meditation experience, not assented to or glossed over. If we really want to attain enlightenment, we must honestly face the immediate realities of our situation. Only then will we understand how bliss may be attained, and what its nature is. Thus the first text weens the aspirant from his basic delusions and attachments, while the second helps disabuse him of the more subtle residues of ignorance.

The emphasis of these texts on sound preparation, logical development, and the avoidance of absolutising any stage (or kind) of meditation into some fixed, static 'goal', should help to forestall any ill-formed characterizations of Buddhist Tantrism. The Vajrayāna does not deny the Hīnayāna or Mahāyāna paths, but goes beyond them to achieve their culmination and ultimate fruition. It is not merely compatible with them, it *requires* them and provides a thorough and final complement to them. Characterizations of the Vajrayāna as violating 'true' Buddhist principles (and hence, as reprehensible), or as being 'liberated' (and hence, fashionable), or as exclusively involving any particular kind of activity or experience, are, to put it honestly, absurd.

Lama Mi-pham's own life should serve to dismiss one-sided views of the Vajrayāna. He was a spiritual and intellectual leader of Tibet in the 19th century, and his status resulted directly from his vigorous mastery of traditional doctrine and practice, coupled to an all-embracing curiosity and creativity that mark a "Renaissance Man." Experimentation and treatises concerning poetry, painting, song, sculpture, dance engineering, chemistry and alchemy accompany the more than thirty-five volumes he wrote on logic, philosophy, Tantra and astrology. The present two texts can only barely suggest the influence his translated writings could have on Western culture and on individuals seeking a basis for hope or a path to enlightenment.

Tibetan texts are typically very terse statements of complex, multi-leveled indications. We want this text to have relevance for beginners as well as experienced meditators, and have therefore avoided the many qualifications and alternative phrasings which a complete presentation would require. We hope these translations and commentaries will suggest the many-faceted expressions of the original Tibetan while steering clear of ambiguities. Much more should be done; this is our effort for the present.

Mangalam

HOMAGE TO MANJUŚRĪ!

Manjuśrī holds the flaming sword of discrimination in his right hand. The sword cuts away the obstacles to meditation, attachments and aversions, wandering thought and conceptualisation, laziness and impatience, leaving only the shining object of concentration. In his left hand he holds the Mahāyāna Sūtras in which the Perfection of Discriminating Awareness is described. His ornaments indicate his attainment of perfect generosity, moral action, patience, perseverance, meditation and discriminating awareness. His Bodhisattva crown shows that he has transmuted the five poisons into the five Buddhawisdoms.

Part One

THE WHEEL
OF
ANALYTIC
MEDITATION

Introduction

The individual who commits himself to a life of self-discovery and selfless service is called a Bodhisattva. The Bodhisattva discovers in himself the source of the complete mental attitude that cuts the root of all anxiety. When the questions, "Who am I?", "Why am I here?" and "What direction should I take?" have been resolved through understanding, difficulties in communication and in manifest fulfillment are swept away. The final mental attitude is described in six aspects (pāramitā): generosity, morality, patience, perseverance, meditation and discriminating awareness. The development of these qualities is the Path of the Bodhisattva.

THE PATH OF THE BODHISATTVA

A necessary precondition for entering the path is an intuitive assurance that the Six Pāramitās describe the attitude of the man most attuned to the needs and responsibilities of the human condition. The desire for these qualities is expressed as immediately fulfilled prayer, transforming whatever emotional vibration is present into joyful detachment. The practice of this final achievement is a constant stream of spontaneous compassion.

The perfection of generosity is the absence of self-ishly motivated action and its replacement by the warmth of giving material goods to alleviate worldly needs, giving security and safety to fearful and timid beings, and giving the highest, most sublime gift which is the Dharma itself. This last act of giving is what the Bodhisattva aims to do continuously. He may do it in many different ways: by sharing a source of inspiration, by teaching the science of mind and meditation, by exemplary action and by expressing the inner recesses of his mind. The gift of a loving vibration to whoever is in need of it, the gift of empathy and self-surrender in menacing confrontation, the gift of affectionate humor in times of self-pity, this is the Bodhisattva's generosity. Without generosity there is only poverty, dejection and a cramped mental attitude in which progress toward total awareness is impossible.

The perfection of morality is the rejection of whatever leads oneself and others away from a positively creative or virtuous state of mind and the cultivation of whatever leads out of a destructive or vicious state of mind. We cannot fix a rigid moral code to guide us because every situation must be approached with openness. However, the ten vices listed by the tradition give fundamental direction as to what to avoid and their antitheses indicate what to cultivate. The ten vices are killing, stealing, sexual misconduct, lying, gossiping, slandering, speaking harshly, coveting, bearing malice and erroneous views, that is, bigotry. Consideration for the well-being of both oneself and others is the touchstone by which any action is judged. Rejection of convention is no virtue while the outrageous, rude, and offensive is only ignorance. Blind devotion should not obscure the distinction between discourtesy and skillful means which sometimes manifests as extraordinary behavior. No realisation or insight removes the value of the refinements of human communication or the civilities and courtesies of prosaic discourse or gives licence to trample others on the path. It is wise to remember that the idiosyncracies of religious hierarchs do not always reflect the spirit of the Dharma. Without the practice of ethics and morality there is great danger of rebirth in a lower realm requiring external assistance for extrication.

The perfection of patience is the antidote to anger and other states of mind which have aversion as their root. Anger arises when the inability to see that the frustration from which anger arises in others is identical with one's own suffering. Anger arises when preconceived expectations are not met. Patience is the virtue which controls the arising of rage and increases the tranquility of mind. The stimulus to anger is a benefactor which provides the opportunity to examine the nature of mind, the cause of passion and the essential baselessness of the attitude. Patience is also acceptance of the results of self-sacrifice of possessions, wealth, time, reputation and even body and limb. Patience is the sandal which the wise man ties to his feet rather than cover the whole road with leather. At first it is not possible to pacify every disturbance and aggression but with concentrated effort patience can be achieved.

The perfection of perseverance is the liberated jet of high energy which destroys obstructing forces. This energy depends upon the banishment of all kinds of laziness. Mental inertia which leads to drowsiness, dreaminess and sleep, depression and dejection which paralyses and turns the mind black and heavy, addiction to power and wealth which causes a stupor of worry and narrow-minded corpulence, all downward-pulling forces are easily dissolved with the energy produced through the cultivation and creative direction of good karmic influences. It is not sufficient to be capable of high-energy bursts; one must possess the drive which persists no matter what forces are in opposition. Persistence is required more in mind-training than in body-training for the subtle grooves in which mind moves are the result of an infinite number of mental actions, well ingrained and therefore requiring much effort to remold.

The perfection of meditation keeps the mind alert and poised, constantly attending to the state of mind. It is the key to developing both the four previously mentioned perfections which comprise the mode of the Bodhisattva's action, and the following perfection of discriminating awareness which is the Bodhisattva's understanding. Meditation is the means by which the ultimate power of understanding and the relative power of mind-control are attained. Meditation practice includes the development of composure (śamatha) and insight (vipaśyanā), the basis of further progress. These practices involve a withdrawal of mind from its functions and its emotional entanglements and conceptualisations. Thus, it is brought to union with the irreducible basis of all name and form. Inseparable from the Emptiness which permeates all things, there arises a feeling of co-naturality, an intuition of oneness with other people

32

from which flows a stream of generous, moral, patient and persevering activity. The feeling tone of this experience is joy. The preparatory purification exercises, the stages of composure and insight, and the stages of vision as the mind becomes increasingly alert are presented in the body of this manual as they are described in the Sūtras and Mādhyamika texts.

The perfection of discriminating awareness occurs when flights of fancy, intellectual conceptualisation and all thought dissolve into an awareness of the skillful means employed in the other five perfections. This understanding cannot be separated from the object of perception which is seen in detail in its luminous reality. The screen of preconceptions and irrelevant associations is torn down by concentration accompanied by a critical dialectic. All theories about the universe are destroyed by the Mādhyamika dialectic which reduces to absurdity each successive machination of the intellect as it is driven from one untenable position to another. Finally, it is forced to let go, allowing the innate understanding of every perception to attune the enlightened mind to the harmony of the total situation.

THE PRACTICE OF MEDITATION

Meditation should be practised regularly and frequently. Sunrise and sunset are the best times for meditation if one is in harmony with natural rhythms. In the city it is better to wait in the evenings until the noise and pace has slowed. After practice has advanced, one-hour periods in the morning and evening can be extended to two-hour periods, a session in the middle of the day, or any time one's life style permits.

Concentration can be achieved most quickly by eliminating external distractions. Noise should be shut out, ill-fitting or harsh-textured clothing should not be worn, the temperature should be neither too hot nor too cold, and visual distractions should be reduced as much as possible. Meditation becomes more difficult when the mind is possessed by emotional problems or problems of living. It is better to begin the practice when the mind is relatively free from distracting worry. Meditation will progress faster in a natural environment. The desert, the mountains, the ocean or wherever there is a sense of vast space is ideal for practice.

Meditation should be practised in the most comfortable position. Although the full-lotus position is most conducive to a perfect relaxation of the body and the nervous system, Western habits of eating, sleeping and physical exercise permit only rare individuals to use this position. Buddhadharma does not stress the necessity of physical prowess. However, the back should be kept straight and the solar plexus thrust forward and relaxed. Place the legs in whatever position is comfortable for an hour's unmoving meditation. A cushion under the buttocks reduces pain and allows greater ease for the legs. Hands should be placed on the knees or on top of one another below the navel. It is most important that the muscles of the body be relaxed. The eyes slightly open should focus about five feet to the front, but if there is visual distraction they should be closed. Breathe naturally. Concentration on the breathing is a meditation practice in its own right which becomes a distraction in the technique presented here. If the nose is stuffed, then breathe through the mouth. Oral breathing develops the qualities of the throat.

When comfortably seated a meditative attitude should be created. Particularly upon awakening, the mind is sluggish and unwieldly and needs lubrication. This is done by devotional exercises. First, refuge is taken:

> I take refuge in the Buddha.
> I take refuge in the Dharma.
> I take refuge in the Sangha.
> (Repeat three times)

This is the traditional formula used by aspirants throughout the world of Buddhadharma to dissolve selfishness in the supreme image of perfection. Taking refuge in the Buddha means the sacrifice of all selfishness and the dissolution of all passion and preconception in the void-bliss which is the nature of being. Taking refuge in the Dharma means following the path which the Bodhisattva must tread from his initial awakening to reality, to manifestation of perfect action and virtue. Practice follows the precepts of the Guru as written down in the Sūtras or received by word of mouth from a personal teacher. Taking refuge in the Sangha means revealing to the world one's aspirations and achievements and relating to others according to the Bodhisattva vow to work for both oneself and others constantly. Reciting and pondering upon the meaning of the Buddha, Dharma and Sangha should have the effect of reawakening the aspiration to retain a vision fleetingly beheld. It should strengthen the motivation for meditation and the means that has been decided upon to attain it. It should recall the brotherhood of fellow practitioners of the past, present and future having the same dedication. If the recitation of these lines becomes a mere formality, meditation will not have been fruitful, while successful meditation will give these words evocative power and sanctity.

The accent in Mahāyāna is 'for others'. The fragile lifeline from the lower realms to the upper breaks only when a selfish climber fears that the rope will not hold due to the number of sufferers clinging to it. Before the practice, the merit which it produces is dedicated to others.

I reserve the positive vibration which this practice creates for the benefit of others.

The possible obstruction of selfishness during the meditation is removed.

After these two devotional exercises one should begin the meditation described in the text, the examination of the image of desire. This should be done without consulting the text, which should be thoroughly studied and reflected upon beforehand. It is best to have a clear grounding in the meaning of the 'components of bodymind' and other terms used in the Abhidharma to describe the process of perception so that meditation may proceed faster. The Abhidharma contains the accretion of thought pertaining to mental functions which successive generations of practitioners have discovered. The contemporary aspirant should take full advantage of the heritage of the tradition.

An initial three-month intensive period of meditation should be sufficient to ground the practitioner in the meaning of the meditation. The first two weeks of practice should be devoted to the analysis of the image of desire which leads to insight into the composite nature of all things. The second two weeks should be devoted to contemplation of transience, the third to contemplation of suffering and the fourth two-week period to contemplation of insubstantiality and self-lessness. The remaining month should be used to develop the understanding of whichever of these four has produced the most advantage in preparation for concentration and insight meditation.

At the beginning of this practice the whole of any meditation session will be involved with discursive analysis and examination and contemplation. According to variation of both external environment and internal obstacles in each individual, results will show sooner or later. The changes in vision of reality indicated in the text will assure the practitioner that progress is being made. The realisation issuing from insight into reality as composite, transient, the origin of suffering and essenceless is the basis for the concentration and insight which arises from constant attention to mind. The amount of time spent on contemplation of the Four Marks of Conditioned Existence gradually becomes reduced as the realisation is induced more rapidly.

When this discursive meditation has ended in the realisation of another kind of awareness of reality and the stream of thought conveying this new vision has vanished, composure meditation begins in concentration. This is called śamatha in Sanskrit and zhi-gnas (pronounced zhinay) in Tibetan. It is meditation upon the mind itself, beginning with fixation and ending in one-pointed absorption as described in the Nine Stages of Meditation enumerated later in the text. As practice of this concentration develops, it will become possible to remain for the entire session or for as long as is desirable in a state of complete absorption. Concentration produces calmness and serenity which is what the Tibetan word zhi-gnas means.

The final level of the nine stages of meditation is consummation of the practice of concentration in outgoing insight. This is called vipaśyanā or lhag-mthong (pronounced lhaktong) which is a clear mind with an incisive insight into the nature of reality. It is this state which can be continued throughout the intervening periods of activity within the world. Calmness and clarity allow the mind freedom from the world of desire and are the basis of the higher meditation which is described in the second text entitled "Instructions on the Ultimate Reality of the Middle Way."

PRIMARY OBSTACLES IN MEDITATION AND THEIR ANTIDOTES

The difficulties of achieving the acute and adaptable mentality which meditation can induce vary according to the individual's problems. An experienced friend may advise upon these, but there are five main obstacles to a consistently concentrated mind which will trouble every beginner.

The first is laziness. Meditation cannot begin unless

there is sufficient energy to get out of bed in time to practise. Cold water and physical exercise can stir the energy necessary to sit and begin a disciplined procedure. Laziness continues to plague the practitioner during meditation. Until the benefit of inner energy is attained, raw will is needed to overcome the temptations of sleep or an early finish. Until the rewards of perseverance strengthen the desire to persist in practice, laziness is always present to drag consciousness below the threshold of worthwhile application. It is laziness which tempts one away with the promise of greater rewards in some sensual paradise and laziness which deludes mind to believe in the efficacy of sleep as the universal panacea.

The antidote to laziness is the complex attitude consisting of exertion supported by aspiration and confidence. Listening to a friend or master with experience in practice discuss the human situation in terms of personal experience and having the benefit of seeing the results of meditation in another person can be highly efficient in providing the continuing aspiration required. The Sūtras are another source of confidence in practice. Whatever increases the desire to meditate should be cultivated at every possible opportunity so that laziness is replaced by the natural inclination to pursue goals that support the endeavor to attain Buddhahood.

The second obstacle is failure to remember instructions. Having sat down in a comfortable position without the text which explains the procedure, it is very easy to forget the details of the meditation practice. It is even easier to pervert the precise instructions in favor of a personal inspiration. The image which is the object of analysis, the aspect of the stream of consciousness, the form of the visualization, the mind which remains elusive, whatever has been prescribed as the object of meditation should be borne in mind constantly. Forgetting the object of meditation renders practice useless, but nonetheless this forgetting is very common in the initial stages of practice. Remember that forceful control is a waste of energy. There is no need to become discouraged by the failure to remember instructions. The antidote is perseverance supported by aspiration which destroys the cloud of indolence. Memory improves as the meditation progresses.

Laziness and forgetfulness are the two primary obstacles to beginning practice. After application has increased to the point of concentration, two other tendencies must be rejected. The third obstacle and the first of these self-defeating tendencies is a numbness of mind. This may even appear to be a kind of samādhi but it is quite unproductive. The object of concentration remains constantly in mind, no distraction arises and the state may be mistaken for peace of mind. The beginner can be assured that if no distractions of thought, feeling or any sensory perception occur then it is inertia rather than calm that is dominant. Nothing can be gained in a drowsy state of composure. The fourth obstacle (the second of these tendencies) is restlessness. The mind wanders constantly in a state of excitement fascinated by the forms which possess it. Distractions dominate. Perception may be very clear and acute but the object of concentration remains like a candle flame to an encircling moth. The antidote to both these conditions is presence of mind. Attentiveness should prohibit either a lapse into interior numbness or a foray into exterior attraction. Forewarned of these two tendencies and keeping the mind constantly attentive to the dangers of either extreme, neither inertia nor restlessness should prevent the fruits of meditation from maturing.

The fifth obstacle is excessive forcefulness in concentration. There is no way in which the door of serenity can be forced. Just as a panicking crowd does violence to itself when it forces its way through a single, small exit, so mind is bruised and hurt when it is forced prematurely toward a goal that can only be attained by relaxation. In trying to relieve the pressure of the slough beneath consciousness, forceful repression of mental monsters is as unproductive as forceful production of them. Equanimity and patience will bring the quickest and most valuable consequences. There is always a point of balance revealing the Middle Way most close to reality and the achievement of complete freedom.

It is very easy to remember the names of these obstacles but it is difficult to recognise them when they occur during practice. The intellect, fearful of its demise, in an orgy of pure sensation, produces the most subtle and deceptive arguments against right meditation as well as the most facile and winningly simple objections to practice. It is of great value to talk with a friend who can explain how to express the experiences encountered during meditation. Once an obstacle is named and clearly defined its destruction is imminent. If it remains an indistinguishable, threatening cloud kept darkly in secret, no progress in practice will be achieved.

41

THE WHEEL OF ANALYTIC MEDITATION

Root Verses

1

*The cause of confusion and frustration in life
Is the virulent passion of the mind.
Distortion and dispersion, the causes of passion,
Must be replaced by incisive attentiveness.*

METHOD OF MEDITATION

2

*Imagining an image before one
Of whatever is desired most
And distinguishing the five groupings of elements
Begin to analyse the imaginary body.*

3

Flesh, blood, bones, marrow, fat and limbs,
Sense organs, internal organs and cavities,
Faeces, urine, worms, hair and nails—
Distinguish the foul parts of the body.

4

Categorise and classify these parts
By composition and sensory field.
Then divide and analyse them
To irreducible particles.

5

Looking for arising desire for any part,
See this 'body' as nothing but foul fragments.
Remember it as a dirty machine or frothing scum,
Or a heap of sticks, stones and pus.

6

When this flow of insight ceases,
Examine the nature, the composite complexity,
Of feeling and conceptualisation,
Reaction associations and consciousness.

7

Seeing the image as a bubble or mirage,
A banana tree or magical illusion,
There will be no desire for it.
So let the stream of insight flow until it vanishes.

Do not attempt to prolong the glow
But proceed and examine another image
So that all corrupted perceptions
Are seen as unfounded fabrications.

9

Watching these baseless fabrications,
Seeing insubstantial phenomena arise
Only to dissolve in an instant,
Is the right way of contemplation.

10

Aware that all worlds of the past have perished
And deducing the inevitable decay
Of the worlds of the present and future,
Discover the cause of suffering in conditioned existence.

11

Knowing that all creatures are born to die
Suddenly and alone
And that all forms of life go through changes,
Look at the transience of the fabric of existence.

12

In short, whatever forms exist,
Impermanent and transitory,
Are illuminated in contemplation
By the power of each mind.

13

As each synthetic desire-image arises,
Shimmering like a bubble, cloud or lightning flash,
Let the stream of insight flow
Enlightening until it vanishes.

14

Then, in the complex multiplicity of becoming
Watch each momentary state of the flux
For the nature of inherent suffering
And the illusive pleasure that will surely
Become subsequent suffering.
Contemplate to capacity
All the pain of the human condition,
The bodymind contrivance as the basis of it all.

15

Through this intrinsic defect of bodymind
Not even so much as a needlepoint
Of its alloyed fabric is free
From the taint of suffering.

16

So it is called the origin of suffering,
A foul sewer, a fiery pit
Or a cannibal island.
Retain this realisation until it fades.

With final insight into suffering
Search in this complex, transient heap
For whatever is thought to be 'I',
Seeing it to be empty of self.

18

Like a waterfall or shower of rain
Or like an empty house,
Let the state of certainty
Stay until it vanishes.

19

When this realisation fades,
Examine methodically as before.
Watch a suitable diversity of images
Sometimes ignoring the precedent order.

20

Searching for the meaning again and again
Sometimes look at others' constitutions
Sometimes investigate one's own contrivance
And sometimes examine all of conditioned existence.

21

So all attachment is broken. In brief,
Rejecting all thought but this fourfold examining—
Diversity, transience, pain and Emptiness—
Constantly turn this wheel of meditation.

22

Directing the clear light of understanding
Upon every kind of distorted image,
The unbroken stream of practice increases
Like a raging prairie fire.

23

Throughout all previous lives, the 'I',
Distorting, obscuring and scattering,
Created a stream of daydreams and mistakes.
Composure must replace that delusion.

24

When scattered energy has been consumed,
And the antidote, examining mind, is still,
When no obstruction arises in mind,
Relax in equilibrium.

25

With the revival of mental activity
Continue analysis as before.
Always keep presence of mind
And mindfulness of the realisation.

26

When one becomes forgetful
And passion arises,
Take this examining to it
As a sword to an enemy.

Practice of watchful examining,
Like a light in darkness
Destroys the last vestiges
Of injurious passion.

28

Insofar as imperfection is understood
And conditioned human nature seen as it is,
So the utmost serenity is known
And the sheer purity of the Great Beyond.

PROGRESS ALONG THE PATH

29

Recognising through constant meditation
The complexity and the transience,
The pain and the absence of substance
Of all conditioned existence, own and other's
bodyminds,

30

Mind is imbued with full comprehension
And even without effort,
When vision is phantasmal,
The head of passion is subdued.

31

Free from the breakers of passion,
The ocean of mind is unruffled and clear.
Attuned to self-possessed purity,
Concentration in peace and calm are gained.

32

One-pointed absorption in mind
Diffuses in piercing insight.
This is the way of initiation,
The common door to the three careers.

SIGNIFICANCE OF ACHIEVEMENT

33

Arising in mutual dependence, seen as magical illusion,
All things are primordially unborn,
Essentially Empty, with no substantial base,
Free from the extreme of the one or the many.

34

With realisation of indivisible space,
All things identified, the Womb of Buddha Bliss,
Beyond confusing existence and peaceful cessation,
All pervasive is the Great Transcendence of Suffering.

Supremely pure and blissful,
It is called the Great Unconditioned.
Here, the attribute of the Great Self
Is unsurpassed and transcendent.

36

In the Tantras, Ati, Anu and Mahāyoga,
Great Bliss and Pure Space come together
In spontaneity of simple understanding,
Thereupon, completing the path.

37

Following the instruction of a Buddha Lama,
Practice the initial purification of the common path
Of both Sūtra and Mantra Mahāyāna
In the tradition of Direct Revelation of
*   the Great Perfection.*

38

Withdraw from the bewilderment of conditioning
On this excellent path of mindfulness.
First by virtue of examination
Passionate reactions no longer occur.
Then with certainty in the Emptiness of bodymind,
All desire for the three worlds is destroyed.

Gradually all trace of delusion
Vanishes into the relief of Emptiness
And dispensing with the antidote of rejection,
All 'I' and 'mine' is finally destroyed.

40

Clinging to nothing, but aspiring to compassion,
Like a bird in the sky of simplicity,
Gliding through life without fear,
The Buddha-son reaches the highest plane.

41

In the teaching of the Noble Tradition
This purification by mindfulness,
Preparation of calm and clarity,
Has crucial stress in the three careers.

42

In continuous practice of inspecting mind,
Purifying through examination,
And finding the smallest of obstacles,
The slightest trace of passion,

43

Scrutiny facilitates serenity.
Just as gold when purified by fire
Becomes malleable, soft and pliant,
So mind, freed from desire, is made responsive.

44

In the Sūtras it is said that
Ritual offering to the Triple Gem
For a thousand years of a god,
Is less beneficial than recognition
Of transience, Emptiness, and selflessness
For the instant of a finger snap.

45

Expressing the fourfold truth of the Mahāyāna
And explaining the eighty-four thousand topics
Are equal in value, said the Buddha.
Meditating upon the meaning of this teaching
Essentially identical to innumerable Sūtras,
Then committing oneself to this form of practice,
A vast source of knowledge is easily found
Leading rapidly to liberation.

46

By virtue of this explanation
And by power of the nectar of detachment
May all beings suffering these painful times
Attain a state of peacefulness.

These verses were written by Mi-pham rNam-par
rGyal-ba in the Iron Hare year [1891]
on the eighteenth day of the month of the Pleiades.
May all beings be happy!

Commentary

VERSE 1

The cause of confusion and frustration in life . . .

The cause of our frustrations, failings, misfortunes and anxieties is not external. It is to be found within. The confusion of emotional conflict dependent upon distorting vagaries of the mind is the primary obstacle to an understanding of Saṃsāra as Nirvāna. Discipline of the mind, concentrating it upon each moment of perception, leads to insight into its nature and its function. Thus, emotional confusion is eliminated.

The truth of suffering is expressed in the recognition of unfulfillment, failure to realise our innate perfection, and the difficulties which are encountered in life. The truth of the cause of suffering is expressed in the recognition of the obscuring nature of passion and the mental process which gives rise to it. The truth of the cessation of suffering is discovered at the end of the path which begins with the discipline of purification by examination and contemplation of mind and leads to mindfulness.

The veil of passion prevents clarity of mind. The word passion (nyon.mongs., kleśa) should be understood in its broadest sense. It refers to emotional forces colouring mind with a dark weight of confusion. It produces a jaundiced outlook. It is always accompanied by mental pain. Tradition distinguishes six tones of passion, each of which is dominated by a particular emotion. The first is stupor, a state of confusion and bewilderment and ignorance. The second is desire, ranging from attraction to pleasure to violent physical lust. The third is hatred, aversion to menacing objects, fear and paranoid rage. The fourth is egoistic pride, limiting, selfish and aggressive. The fifth is equivocation prohibiting certainty and decision, creating doubt and fear. The sixth is abstract conceptualisation unrelated to immediate sensory perception. The ramifications of these six describe the whole gamut of passion which impedes the development of the Bodhisattva ideal.

Lustful passion, which is the expression of the animal instinct to copulate and which may produce anything from bitter disappointment to an illusion of ecstasy is only one form of passion to which the text refers. Like the other feeling tones of passion, it is characterized by an overweening impulse to attain a state which is not existent in the present moment. Any interruption in the act of copulation is a potential source of severe irritation and anger. The emotion is an all-consuming drive to attain what is not. Dissatisfaction with the state of mind as it is, is the necessary precondition to lust. Jealousy, hatred, pride—all the innumerable combinations and shades of emotion are overwhelming in their power. When under the effect of one of these it is difficult but not impossible to understand what the devil is, where it came from and how it arose. Passion is the strength of the emotion which destroys clarity and serenity. All forms of passion are inherent in the bodymind composition and are traces of dispositions which belong to a lower form of consciousness. Dominated by any one of them, the wonder and precious beauty of immediate experience is missed, and understanding of the path, which leads from birth to rebirth and eventually out of the cycle of becoming, is lost.

The veil of misunderstanding is the ground of passion. Limiting views about the nature of the universe and one's own identity cause conflict between what exists in reality and what one would wish to be. So long as one is preoccupied with the apparent difference between the reality and the dream, there can be no harmony between the external and internal, the macrocosm and the microcosm. Preconceptions prevent spontaneous action. Lack of a complete knowledge of one's identity results in constant failure to take advantage of opportunities and causes the stream to flow by—rather than through—the mind. Like a house of cards, preconception collapses under stress leaving a fearful vacuum to be filled by whatever poison habitual reaction envenoms. Conceiving anew, without understanding what is real and what is not, dreaming fantastic improbabilities, wishful thinking again results in disappointment and accompanying confusion. So round and round from rebirth to rebirth, never finding the solace of peaceful clarity, despair deepening with frenetic grasping at straws in the wind, there is only suffering.

Habitual reaction patterns are hard to break. The difficulty of changing the subtle and deeply ingrained

57

reactions of mind is far greater than breaking the gross habits of body such as tobacco smoking. Although one is darkly aware that preconceptions and prejudices colour reaction and judgment, until practice or a lucid moment illuminates, only this blurred conviction of something awry within the mind keeps aspiration alive. Constant practice of the other aspects of the ideal attitude loosens the mind from the heavier fetters. With growing understanding of the laws of Karma, of cause and effect in our lives, the mist rises from the mindscape sufficiently to give a glimpse of the location of the path. This meditation puts the aspirant surely on the path.

METHOD OF MEDITATION

VERSES 2 - 5

Imagining an image before one . . .

The search for the nature of reality begins with the visualisation of the most fascinating object of sexual desire. Men should take a woman as the object of meditation, women should take a man, and homosexuals one of their own sex. This situation should be divided into the five groupings of bodymind constituents (phung.po.lnga., pañcaskandha). The mental object is fixed by the faculty of mind which tends to lock into a perceptual situation (dpyod.pa., vicāra) while the discursive faculty of mind (rtog.pa., vitarka)

thoroughly examines it. The search is for both the external base of desire for the sex object and for something substantial or self-existent in the world of created things, the elements of which are collected together under one of the groups of bodymind constituents.

For a man, a woman is taken as the object of
examination because she evokes the strongest emotional response in the mind. She is the giver of sexual
satiety, she is the comforter, the mother, she is the
origin of much energy. In youth particularly, the natural desire for a sexual partner, a mate with whom to
procreate, is the dominant instinct. Woman is taken as
the epitome of desirability, the strongest attachment
of mind in the world of desire from which this meditation will lead.

Lust, which should not be confused with sexuality,
is compared first to a honeyed razorblade which the
foolish man, ignorant of the laws of karmic cause and
effect, licks with his stupid tongue. Secondly, it is
compared to the poison apple which looks so rosy and
edible to the gullible but which is the cause of painful
sickness. The man or woman that has his or her tongue
lacerated is likely to refrain from a second attempt at
savouring the honey, but the unfortunate who tastes
the poisoned apple has no sure means of determining
the source of the poison, and without a warning or an
introduction to the honeyed razorblade, is likely to
wallow in the juices of his own passion for many lifetimes.

In order to practise this meditation a healthy aspiration to be free from the fetters of attachment
which lust and desire impose should have arisen.
Whoever is not disillusioned with the romantic and

59

sensual ideal that popular culture implants at an early age, is karmically ordained to wander in the world of desire until maturity brings revulsion. Disillusionment may occur through an experience of pain in failing to attain the lasting contentment which has been promised either in sexual or romantic attachment. The aspiration towards freedom, besides being a wish to get out of that pain, should also be a wish to remain constantly in the transcendent state of pure awareness which may have been experienced at a peak moment with or without a sexual partner.

The tradition has used the five groupings of body-mind constituents in listing all the elements of existence. These categories are form (gzugs., rūpa), feeling (tshor.ba., vedanā), conceptualisation ('du.shes., saṃjñā), reaction associations ('du.byed., saṃskāra), and consciousness (rnam.shes., vijñāna).

The instructions above show how to analyse the desired body in terms of the first grouping of form. First, one dissects the body into its component parts. This reveals 'flesh, blood, bones . . .' and so on as listed in the text. One should carefully picture to oneself each separate bodily part and observe whether or not desire arises for any of these.

The analysis is continued by breaking down these bodily parts into their constituents. Here, we arrive at the basic material substances of physical nature. Buddhist philosophy begins, like modern science, by conceiving of material objects as made up of atomic particles. The traditional Buddhist account is a rather complex system of combinations of four basic kinds of atoms. These four are earth, air, fire and water representing the qualities of density, motility, temperature and cohesion. The essential point to note in the course of the analytic meditation is that physical objects are compounded of various kinds of tiny particles. As before, one should observe whether or not there is any desire for these particles in themselves.

So far, the analysis has revealed that external objects, when thought of as physical and corporeal, are found to be compounded of parts and that these parts are themselves reducible to atomic particles. Now we turn the analysis to the compound nature of the individual's sensory and mental experience of the object. One should recall the five kinds of sensory experience thinking of each as composed of three elements—the organ of perception, the sense field and the corresponding awareness of the object. The following diagram represents this:

SENSE ORGAN	SENSE FIELD	CORRESPONDING OBJECT-AWARENESS
1. eye	form and colour	Awareness of form and colour
2. ear	sound	Awareness of sound
3. nose	smell	Awareness of smell
4. tongue	taste	Awareness of taste
5. body	touch	Awareness of touch

Thus, the sensory experience is divided into five organs of sense, five sense fields, and five corresponding sorts of mental impression. Mental activity is likewise given this threefold division. As the faculty of mentation, it is grouped with the sense organs. As its field it has the data presented by the five senses and all other mental events (memories, feelings, ideas and so on). The mind selects and synthesises the sense data and residual associations producing our orientation toward the situation.

In this way, we should analyse the experience of the desired body. This experience is compounded of eighteen elements, three for each of the five senses and three for mind. As a perceived object, the body enters the five sense fields. It should be examined in each of the five ways it is sensed. Each of the five senses should be thought of as a combination of three elements as explained above. One should note that our experience of the object is wholly dependent upon the proper functioning of the five senses and upon the presence of the cognising mind. Next, one should recall how the bare sense data is processed by the mind. Various factors (such as memory, attention, etc.) are constantly operating, selecting the data and evaluating. These factors are further discussed in the next section with reference to the other four groupings of bodymind constituents.

The result of this examination is the realisation that there is nothing desirable in itself in the body of the person. All apparently desirable features are found not to be desirable when broken down into component parts. But more important is the discovery that this external object, a body, is a compound construct dependent upon the senses and the mind for its existence. It is necessary to cultivate the understanding of all 'external' objects as dependent upon the five senses and the perceiving mind. The illusion of self-contained entities existing apart from the process of per-

ception must be destroyed. After other external objects and one's own body have been examined, the
material universe will be seen to be compounded,
fabricated, composite and multiple. In this way we
begin to understand the composite nature of all things,
the first of the Four Marks.

VERSES 6 - 8

When this flow of insight ceases . . .

Faced with failure to discover something substantial and continuously rewarding in the most desirable
exterior attraction, the search turns inward in an
examination of the mind. In the mind can be discovered the cause of the mistaken notion of the
desired person and whether or not there is any essential substance that can be relied upon to give continuous contentment. This mental field which is the
result of cooperation between the mind and its functions producing cognition of mental objects is the sixth
of the triads of elements. All that is finite in the mind
can be categorised under the divisions of this mental
field. Tradition recognises various stages in the process
of perception. Feeling arises first, then the mental
impression or concept, followed by reaction associations, all inseparable from the consciousness which
cognises.
    Every perception is accompanied by an immediate
feeling of pleasure, pain or indifference. This emotional response (vedanāskandha) has the function of

the gatekeeper. Whatever is pleasant tends to be accepted and whatever is unpleasant tends to be rejected. The evaluation into good and bad is made at the beginning of the mental process. The judgment is determined by earlier experiences, conditioning, the actions of past lives. Sometimes it is a useful appraisal as, for example, when the unpleasant sensation of heat warns against being burnt, but because in past life there has been much ignorance, inappropriate reactions have been ingrained. The alluring body is merely a 'heap of sticks, stones and pus' yet the reaction to it is overwhelming attraction. Mistaking something of limited potential reward for the answer to life's problems is similar to mistaking a rope for a snake. Thorough examination of the feeling tone of such a perception shows the snake to be a rope with a projected feeling tone imposed upon it. Equanimity in the face of all perception allows the unsullied characteristics of every situation to be discovered.

The grouping of concepts and their applications (samjñāskandha) refers to the collection of sensory data as an idea of the object of perception. This is no abstraction but rather a composite sensory impression, an idea of the object in terms of its colour, shape and qualities. It must be understood that this is a composition of many different perceptions and not an intuited image of unity. By labelling the parts and understanding the field of perception in which they originated there can be no mistaking the internally reflected object as being a desirable whole. Without the screen of feeling which filters out the intensity of the immediate perception, this function of mind produces the experience of pure sensation.

The grouping of reaction associations (saṃskāra- skandha) refers to the seed impressions set in the mind as a result of previous experience and brought into play by their associations with the immediate perception. These associations form around the sensation-idea and colour it accordingly. This is the stage at which the object becomes distorted by subjective associations which have the propensity of transforming a rope into a snake. Due to these individual tendencies the same object of perception may be seen by different people as desirable or threatening, beautiful or ugly, black or white. The tradition lists eleven associations which produce a positive state of mind and six root and twenty derivative associations which produce a negative state of mind.

The eleven qualities which produce an attitude conducive to the attainment of Buddhahood are: faith, a confident desire to attain release from the round of birth and death; discretion, discrimination leading to an identification of Saṃsāra and Nirvāṇa; discipline in virtue, the restraint which destroys the path to the lower realms; equanimity, the composure retained under every eventuality; shame, humility in the face of one's own failings; disgust, a communicable empathetic shame for others; detachment, freedom from desire, resentment and distraction; absence of aversion, a patient acceptance of situations we cannot control; alert consciousness, awareness of specific characteristics; absence of aggression, harmlessness and compassion; and sustained effort, perseverance in every sphere.

The six qualities from which all anxiety is derived and which create obstacles to the fulfillment of the

Bodhisattva Vow are: delusion, ignorance of the laws of cause and effect and the Triple Gem; desire, the suffering of attachment to the worlds of sensuality, form and formlessness; hatred, the torment of suffering; pride, arrogance of achievement in conquering fear and having no respect for others; equivocation, uncertainty as to what is true and what is not; and opinionatedness, belief in a limited conceptual framework as all-encompassing.

Twenty negative manifestations arise from the six root vicious associations: violence, malice and rancour, vocal rage, envy, hypocrisy, deceit, shameless self-indulgence, shameless tolerance of others' self-indulgence, repression of desire, ignorance, regret etc., menace and aggression, avarice, self-conceit, trustlessness and lack of aspiration, laziness, indiscretion and indiscriminate sloth, forgetfulness, absence of presence of mind, inertia, languidness and restlessness.

Whichever of these elements are associated with the object of perception due to past action, past experiences and innate tendencies of mind, determine the quality of the final composite image which is presented to consciousness.

The grouping of consciousness (vijnanaskandha) refers to the six kinds of consciousness which illumine the six sensory fields and integrate the composite image processed by feelings, ideas and reaction associations.

This examination resulting in the extinction of the belief that reality is anything but a complex process of interacting elements destroys the inclination to grasp at any part of any object, hoping thereby to attain the elixir of life. It permits the mind to relax in tensionless

enjoyment. After the analytic examination and cate-
gorization has established the nature of the bodymind as an insubstantial compound, the mind need
only contemplate its own functions to perceive the ex-
quisite Emptiness of all phenomena. Right Meditation, the final stage of the Noble Eightfold Path, is
thereby achieved.

VERSES 9 - 13

Watching these baseless fabrications . . .

Although with some reflection it becomes obvious
that nothing is permanent, that everything passes
away in time, that all created things are transient, it is
sometimes more pleasant to delude ourselves into
thinking that the same situation will last. Thus, the
truth of impermanence is forgotten. What should be
done today is postponed until tomorrow. Knowing
that some actions lead to unhappiness and thinking
that the change in habit can be effected later, another
opportunity for doing what results in a more healthy
state is neglected. Unwilling to admit that life may end
in the next instant, no effort is made to make this
instant as perfect as could be. Aware of the importance of meditation and following the precepts of the
teacher, nevertheless practice is ignored and still the
mirror of mind remains clouded. Knowing darkly that
there is an infinity to be experienced in every instant,
still there is no attempt to realise it. Contemplation of
all things, external phenomena, the body and mind

complex, the figments of mind and all, brings constant recognition of the unique chance which is offered to attain realisation of the Buddha Nature now.

This constant recognition and remembrance of the present moment in a state of constant mindfulness should be achieved by watching the rise and fall of perceptions and convincing oneself of the transience of the outer world. The first practice is described in the first verse and is the most rapid way to conviction of the truth of impermanence. After continuous practice there will be an understanding that nothing can be said to exist which is not registered on the screen of the mind. Does a falling tree in the centre of an uninhabited forest make a noise? The Buddha Gautama warned his followers against making any assumptions which were not functions of immediate experience, for preconceptions of any kind are hindrances on the path. In the previous analysis of the components of experience it was discovered that the object of perception is a combination of various sensual impulses and therefore, as every perception is different, the object is recreated every moment. Each image as it arises in the mind is seen as a brilliant flash Empty in nature.

Mindfulness of impermanence is assisted by a discursive examination of external phenomena in commonsense terms. Cliffs falling, mountains eroded, rocks tumbling, earth washed away, is all evidence of the impermanence of the physical environment. Astronomers believe that each solar system and galaxy has a life cycle and that many universes preceded this one. The natural cycles are important objects of contemplation. The seasons change, day turns into night,

the moon has its phases, the seasons are accompanied by life cycles of flora and fauna.

So it is with the human body, achievements and values. Nothing lasts. Few human beings have ever lived beyond two or even one hundred years; no hero, prophet, priest or king could escape death. The remains of civilisations remind of past races and cultures which were inevitably consumed in the passage of time. Culture, customs, and values change from year to year. Wealth changes hands with no apparent cause, and it is impossible to retard the process of change in economic status through miserliness. There is nothing in the realm of human experience which does not change. Emotional states are totally erratic, depending upon the stimulus and the changing karmic stream. Moods of others can be observed changing without any apparent cause.

Knowing that all things will decay and eventually pass away, it is important to realise that the time of that eventual demise is unknown. No one knows the time of his death, whether he will live to a fine old age, whether he will leave a widow and children, whether he will die in his sleep tonight, whether he will be killed on the road this afternoon, or even whether he will live to draw another breath. There can never be any certainty. It is well to remember the ever-present threat of weapons of mass destruction in the hands of men who are ignorant of the laws of karmic cause and effect and the Bodhisattva Vow. It is as uncertain how death will come as when it will come. Death may come by water, earth, fire or air. Considering the various ways in which men have died, insight into the uncertainty of continued existence increases.

With developed understanding of change and decay the connection with suffering becomes obvious. The mental pain which is caused by the uncertainty of existence is the fear of death which is rooted deeply within the mind. After seeing the connection between suffering and transience, the inter-relationship of all the Four Marks of Conditioned Existence can be perceived. Understanding of one of them includes an understanding of them all. The previous investigation of all elements of experience stressed the insubstantiality of composite creation, and impermanence may be inferred from the necessary interaction which is inherent in composition and decomposition.

Full understanding of any of these marks of conditioned existence may stimulate a depth reaction of fear. Meditation is bound to uncover hidden wells of dissatisfaction, for insight into the nature of reality involves a painful process of self-discovery. If the obstacles on the path become too great and the danger of a rejection of the means of meditation presents itself, then advice from an adept master of meditation becomes indispensable. Loss of cherished delusions, failure of ingrained defense mechanisms, and confrontation with the stark reality of human existence are preliminary stages on the way to mastery of every situation to serve both self and others.

VERSES 14 - 16

Then, in the complex multiplicity of becoming . . .

The victorious tradition instructs upon the way to free mind from the bonds of both poles of experience. Both pleasure and pain are forms of suffering to the aspirant who strives to free himself from the round of birth and death. A pleasure which is grasped and clung to is the cause of subsequent suffering. All joy falls away from the height of sensual pleasure if it is hankered after and then grasped and clung to. Unless there is detachment there can be no happiness. The truth of suffering was the first insight which the Buddha Gautama shared with his friends at Sarnath after his enlightenment under the Tree of Life at Bodhagaya. He understood that enmeshed in the warp and woof of mundane love and hate there could be no release from suffering. Love and hate are equally the cause of suffering. The passions which stem from the basic reactions of attraction and aversion are likewise the cause of suffering.

The bodymind confusion is characterised by pain from its conception. After an agonising cramp in the womb for several months, the first reaction to birth is a scream. The pains of growth are punctuated by disease of the bodymind and disease follows one until death. Sickness is suffering. Then after the maturation of the bodymind, decay sets in with its accompanying failure of the senses and the brain in senility until the heart can function no longer and the ultimate pain of death must be suffered. This is the pain of the human condition: embodiment. The bodymind is the form of embodiment. The purity and ecstasy which is inherent within this conditioned frame is forgotten in the pre-occupying pain of its existence.

Getting what is unwanted is suffering; not getting what is wanted is suffering. Losing what is wanted is suffering and keeping what is unwanted is suffering. Even getting what is wanted is suffering when the thrill of possession turns into the grey despondency of regret. Having once known the power and glory of a god, the gradual diminution of that pleasure is most painful. The pride of sexual prowess inevitably becomes the frustration of impotence followed by the sterility of old age. The bodymind has a built-in mechanism ensuring its continual suffering.

Ignorance of the cause of suffering and insistent movement in the same direction compounds suffering. The man who mistakes wealth for the antidote to the suffering of poverty merely replaces one pain by another. The pain of acquisition, of miserliness, of fear of loss may cause a welter of confusion and far greater pain than the original condition. There is no release by replacing one mental state by another, one passion by another, one woman by another, one home by another or one life by another. Change in itself is a cause of suffering, and the belief that by alteration, greater contentment can be found is a potent delusion.

VERSES 17 - 18

With final insight into suffering...

Realisation of this fourth major characteristic has been partially achieved in the search for something substantial in the groups of components of bodymind in which all elements of existence are subsumed and in the search for something permanent. If nothing substantial or permanent is found then identity becomes something extremely elusive. If nothing is found that thinks except the thought and if nothing is found which acts or speaks except the action or the sound and if nothing remains constant except change, there can be nothing to defend and nothing to be afraid. Repetition of these exercises is important because it is very easy to intellectually convince oneself of the truth of the absence of identity or selflessness, but very difficult to experience the result of complete realisation.

There are two stages in the development of this insight. The first is conviction of the external world as a world of vibration known only by the five senses and without a substantial base. Suppose five blind men discover an ox. Touching different parts of its body, each thinks he has found the essential ox. Severing the parts, cooking and eating them, what becomes of the essential ox? The outer world of perception is dependent upon the five senses which are most limited in scope. There is no reason to believe that the reality of existence is so limited. The vision of the world as a shimmering flux of colour and form is the result of breaking the belief in the substantiality of the objects of which the senses give notice.

The second stage is the insight into one's own insubstantiality. After the initial examination of body, it is disheartening to identify with a stinking heap of organic matter, yet nothing in the mind was found to exist for more than the duration of a single perception. What then am 'I'? With growing certainty of one's selflessness, afraid of the void which one faces, many defenses against final acceptance of reality will arise. Each should be examined separately and demolished. The gradual expansion of the vision from the universe being a collection of independently self-existent entities to a field of inter-related, insubstantial vibrations can be painful and should be cautiously practiced.

Insight into the nature of reality as baseless, insubstantial, without an essence is the necessary precedent to understanding Emptiness, the Void which is realised with further practice.

The final insight into suffering which is mentioned in the text refers to a preview of death. The third experience which the Buddha Śakyamuni suffered that turned his mind from family, fame, wealth and success, was knowledge of eventual death. Contemplation of the suffering of the human condition leads to the thought of the final path of withdrawal of consciousness from the body. The result of the failure to find an identity expedites that process and all of the smaller deaths that must be endured between birth and final departure. After the self which grasps is destroyed in meditation, there can be no attachment when final dissolution occurs. There can be no grasping at any object which is taken away and no grasping at any object which comes within reach. There should be no reluctance to give up this body and no temptation to take up another body. In this way this meditation is the practice of dying.

VERSES 19 - 21

When this realisation fades . . .

After each period of practice of any of the four parts of this inspection of mind, a certainty should have arisen with an emotional tone of joy and characterised by a clarity of vision which sees reality according to the similes. This flow of realisation must be made continuous and that is done by repetition of the exercises. The analysis of the elements of experience should be practised upon any object of attachment, not only of desire but of hatred, jealousy, pride and ignorance. In this way there will be a direct attack on all of the basic passions. At the same time, understanding of the process of cognition will remove obstacles and knots in that path.

It is not necessary to practise the four in the same order. After each has been practised a sufficient number of times for one to stand out as the most easily accomplished, concentrate primarily upon that one. Full understanding of one of the Four Marks of Conditioned Existence gives full understanding of them all. Accomplishment in any of these practices leads to peaceful calm and clarity after the discursive examination has ended.

Allowing the stream of mental images to flow, sometimes attention will wander to external objects, sometimes to other people and sometimes to one's own bodymind. Whatever the object of perception, the same search for substantiality should be applied. Whatever emotional tone accompanies perception should be examined to its origin. No other thought should arise except those of the composite nature, the transience, the inherent suffering and the essential insubstantiality of the object of perception.

VERSES 22 - 27

Directing the clear light of understanding . . .

The investigation has become an application of the light of consciousness to whatever enters the mind. As clear perception of the characteristics of phenomena becomes ingrained, the detailed analysis of images becomes unnecessary and mind begins to function automatically to destroy the delusions which have previously obscured the nature of reality.

Past lives are the momentary lifespans of previous mental events, the cycles of prepossession with a particular state of mind, and the duration of time from birth to death of the bodymind complex.

Constant mindfulness guarding the doors of the six senses is the *sine qua non* of entering into the peaceful state. Its practice results in release from the bonds of the sensual realm, the realm of desire in which the mind's grasping tendencies obscure and distort. Mindfulness arises on the foundation of the insight induced by the search for a substantial and permanent entity and the contemplation of the nature of the bodymind complex.

Just as suffering and ignorance compounded itself when mind had no direction, now that consciousness has intentional direction clarity increases like a fire consuming more the hotter it becomes. The habits of lifetimes are destroyed in the intensity of that flame. The 'I' which has reacted with habitual selfishness distorting perception by seeing only what it would like to see, obscuring the reality by larding perception with overtones and associations which have no bearing upon the actuality, and scattering mind by running off in abstract conceptualisation and fantastical daydreams, is destroyed by the intensity of continued focusing of the clear light of understanding.

VERSE 28

Insofar as imperfection is understood . . .

The Great Beyond is the peace at the end of suffering—Nirvāna. Rather than escape from the world's harshness, the Buddhadharma teaches an acceptance of it, a recognition of human inadequacy wherein is discovered the origin that transcends it. Practice of concentration alone without accompanying insight leads to a state of absorption in which the mental functions that produce suffering are held in abeyance. These poison-producing habits of mind continue their

THE
WHEEL OF
ANALYTIC
MEDITATION malevolent operation when mind returns from its absorption in itself into sensory activity, until meditative absorption and phenomenal activity are revealed as identical by penetrating insight.

PROGRESS ALONG THE PATH

VERSES 29 - 32

Recognising through constant meditation . . .

Recognition of the Four Marks of All Phenomena is the foundation of achievement of concentration and understanding. This meditation takes the aspirant to the stage where emotional conflict and disturbing thought-trains are eliminated in a state of concentration called 'peaceful calm'. Phantasmal vision is the consciousness of phenomena as shimmering and insubstantial apparitions. There should be no hallucination at this stage. In this peaceful and calm condition nothing disturbs equanimity whether coming from inside or outside the mind. It is a state untroubled by sensual desire or revulsion. Privation, lack of food or clothing, and adversity of any kind make no impression upon the mind. At the same time the insight which is engendered by one-pointed absorption allows clear vision of one's own mind and the nature of things round about. There is no fantasy, no planning for the future, no mental trips of abstract deduction into the realm of mere possibility, there is only concentration here and now.

This is an initiation into the stream which, like a

mountain creek, eventually flows into the ocean. The peace and calm of this condition is in great contrast to previous experience, but one can become attached to this 'peace and calm'. It is as if a leaking roof has finally been plugged, yet the dampness which remains inside has still to be eliminated. The subtle traces of desire and aversion which belong to the realms of aesthetic form and formlessness remain to be destroyed. Concentration and insight cut gross attachment to the realm of desire, and it is the peace and calm of freedom from that state that is felt after practising this meditation. Yet this is only the beginning of complete understanding of oneself and others and the whole universe and of complete skill in using whatever means are available.

Emotional attachment in the realm of sensuality is the cause of jealousy, prohibiting friendship; pride, maintaining aloof isolation; greed, always reaching outside the immediate; hatred, inflaming and perverting the mind; and plain gross stupidity in sensual sloth. These crass mental tendencies are eliminated once the realm of sensuality has been transcended. The means which the tradition prescribes is examination then concentration and insight.

The three careers which the text mentions are the Śrāvakayāna, Pratyekabuddhayāna and the Bodhisattvayāna. The Śrāvaka is the diligent disciple who suppresses his emotions but, because he cannot understand the nature of reality, remains bound by Saṃsāra. His greatest obstacle is self-doubt. The Pratyekabuddha retires to solitude in his desire to understand himself. Having mastered his passionate nature he succeeds in ridding himself of the delusion that

81

there is something external that is ultimately rewarding. Both Śrāvaka and Pratyekabuddha lack the selfless motivation which distinguishes them from the
Bodhisattva. In order to devote himself to other sentient life, immersed in the world for the sake of
universal harmony, the Bodhisattva has discovered
the essential emptiness of all conditioned existence
throughout the three worlds. Both Hīnayāna and Mahāyāna prescribe concentration and insight meditation as the initial practice on the path. In the Vajrayāna it is only one of innumerable methods which
the adepts have used.

It is well to remember a favorite Indian simile. The
mind is like an ocean—naturally deep, translucent and
boundless. When the currents of passion stir up the
depths and the surface is disturbed by waves of
thought, there is no clarity and no peace. There is only
the clouded churning of the water and nothing else is
known. The natural peace of mind can only be attained if emotional conflict and disturbed thinking are
allayed.

After the practice of the examining meditation
when imaginings and passions no longer afflict the
mind and there is equilibrium, the nine stages of
meditation are passed through to complete calm and
clarity. There should be no break in practice from
examining to fixation. Fixation upon what? The examination drops away by itself as the mind becomes
stilled and concentrated in its own nature. The first
stage of meditation emerges when the tendency of
mind changes from an inclination to trip out to an
inclination to be still (gtod.pa.'jog.pa.). The second
stage is a steadily increasing tendency to remain fixed

in concentration while thoughts, though still arising, have less power of fascination (rgyun.du.'jog.pa.). The third stage is a facility in immediately bringing the mind back into a concentrated state when it tends to wander in imagination or inspection (blan.te.'jog.pa.). Then, the fourth state is a close attention to the nature of mind in which, although distractions may disrupt, only the periphery is affected (nye.ba.'jog.pa.).

With the fifth state of meditation there is a pleasant enjoyment of the achievement of concentration. At the same time there is progressively less grasping, mind becoming looser and less possessive. This relaxation permits the function of foreseeing the future and reading the past. This is the achievement of discipline ('dul.bar.byed.pa.). Desire for amplification and intensification of this experience leads into the sixth state of meditation in which conflicting emotions are resolved in peace. Whatever arises in the state which may potentially produce confusion is immediately dissolved by the power of the antidote of serenity. Revulsion towards flights of fancy, idle speculation and the squalor of the external world arises and this negative force can propel into deep concentration (zhi.bar.byed.pa.). Seeing that the incessant worry and bustle of mundane life are escapable, strong motivations arise for more of the same peace and the seventh state of meditation is entered. In this state of concentration, desire for what is not, together with the accompanying feeling of frustration, is removed. Hereafter there need be neither depression at not attaining what is desired nor any desire for what is not possessed. Traces of dispositional difficulties are dissolved by the antidote of sweet serenity (rnam.

par.zhi.bar.byed.ba.). Then in the eighth state of meditation one-pointedness of mind is achieved and here there is no inclination to return to the external world (rtse.gcig.tu.byed.pa.). The ninth and final state of meditation is a return from one-pointed concentration through the all-pervading substratum of existence into conditioned existence which is now totally illuminated. Whatever arises in mind is like ripples on the surface of the deep, clear and calm ocean (mnyam. par.hjog.par.byed.pa.).

These nine stages are an idealised framework from which the practitioner may gauge his progress toward the completion of the path of Śamatha and Vipaśyanā. This idealised progression is useful as a guide but due to differences of individual disposition rarely will it accord with actual progress. There is a danger that the meditator will be loathe to leave the state of Samādhi or one-pointed concentration at the eighth stage. This is like leaving home to seek a fortune and forgetting the purpose of one's search, becoming fascinated by the places and the people on the way. The insight which brings clarity and freedom from the distortion and heaviness of passionate stupidity only arises in the return from deep concentration. The Bodhisattva's Vow cannot be fulfilled in a state of total withdrawal.

The attainment of the ninth state of meditation is an initiation into the path. Before this initiation it is like waiting to fall in love—never knowing if it will happen, when it will happen, or what its nature will be. Or it is like waiting in the courtyard of a king, craving admittance but having neither the rank nor the wealth or power to enter, knowing that the answer to all problems lies within but ignorant of what will be found.

VERSES 33 - 36

*Arising in mutual dependence, seen as magical
illusion . . .*

The description of this method of meditation has
stated in discursive terms the stages and objects of
examination. Now in this third part the vision of
reality by the purified mind is revealed, showing what
is possible to attain through complete understanding
arising from thorough practice of the instructions.
These first stanzas describe the state of Buddhahood
in both Mahāyāna and Vajrayāna terms. The words
used here are sounds to express the ineffable. It is a
poetic vision attempting to describe what lies beyond
limitation, or rather it is the ultimate attempt of language to go beyond itself. Reality is approached in
four ways. In the first stanza reality is seen as a relative
field of evanescent light in a constant state of flux. In
the second stanza reality is seen as the all-pervasive,
all-permeating, transcendent origin and end of all
things. In the third stanza reality is seen as the unity of
the essentially pure base and the effulgence which
gives apparent form. In the fourth stanza reality is
seen as spontaneous awareness of the immediate actuality.
    Mutual dependence means that nothing arises
without a causal relationship with every element of the
preceding situation and a conditional connection with
every element of the present situation. The universe

has an integral unity which its apparent diversity belies. By holding to one limiting point of view at a time, the necessary relationship with the totality is obscured. Magical illusion is used as a simile, not because it is something produced out of nowhere like a conjurer's trick, but because reality shimmers in its insubstantiality. The magic lies in the everpresent freshness, the astonishing experience of perception of the present moment, and the illusion in the elusive, ungraspable, insubstantial and transient nature of experience.

Everything that exists in both body and mind, inside and outside, has the same primordially unborn nature. Primordial does not mean 'in the beginning of time' but 'at the root of the moment, the essence, the path and the fundamental origin of the situation'. This same nature is described as Empty because it has no characteristics and no quality. It is inconceivable and without bounds. It cannot be called infinite and it certainly is not finite. It is not eternal nor temporal, having no origin and no end. Therefore it is said to be unborn and Empty. This Emptiness is first understood with the insight into the insubstantial character of all elements of experience, both the insubstantial nature of external phenomena and the selflessness of bodymind. Developing this insight, various levels of Emptiness are discovered leading to the Ultimate Reality where no duality disturbs perfect bliss.

This vision is beyond the labels of philosophy. The experience cannot be said to be of unity or plurality. There is no wandering mind to become prepossessed with abstract labelling in the intensity of immediate perception. The nature of reality cannot be defined by any extreme. If the unity is considered absolute then a lack of discrimination of specifics will result and the full richness of experience will remain unopened. If the multiplicity is considered absolute then the mind will be fragmented and tossed about as it finds no integral identity, all the while in danger of identifying with a limited experience creating either fear or pride.

The first verse describes the initial experience of the Middle Way Vision which arises in a clear and calm mind. Developing the vision, the magical form and its Empty base become the Womb of Buddha Bliss. The Tathāgatagarbha is the seed of Buddhahood within all sentient life, the potential perfection which is the realised actuality of Buddha Nature. It is an all-pervasive ground and coincident manifestation of perfection. It is beyond the turmoil and confusion of the experience between birth and death, the suffering of the Wheel of Existence, and it is beyond the peace of cessation which lies at the end of meditation practice. It is called the Great Nirvāṇa (mya.ngan.'das.chen.) or the Great Transcendence of Suffering. The practice which leads to this realisation is the identification of the nature of all things in the same free space.

With continuing grounding in the Womb of Buddha Bliss, purity and serene happiness produce the virtue or attribute of the Buddha which is seen as the complete manifestation of transcendent vibrations of giving, patience, perseverance, moral discipline, meditation and understanding. The Great Self is the realised being who works for the benefit and liberation of all sentient life. The Great Unconditioned is not the absence of phenomenal characteristics and absorption in quietude and detached repose; it is identification with the purity of all things and the experience of all things as blissful, although at the same time it is inseparable from Emptiness. Once the distinction between subject and object has been destroyed, the expression of the vision is necessarily in paradoxical terms.

In the last of these four verses the Vajrayāna, the ultimate vision of reality, is described in terms of immediate spontaneity never straying from the immanent perfection of awareness. The Mahā, Anu and Ati Yogas are the ground, the path and final achievement. Here the vision of the highest Tantras is consummated. Nothing in either life or death destroys the strength of concentration which understands the nature of every situation and experience. Each situation is taken as it arises and is transformed into the nectar which relieves and satisfies the suffering of whoever is in need. Form is seen as the body of the Guru, sound is heard as the voice of the Guru, and thought is absolutely free from abstraction. There is total mastery in the unity of the substance and the manifestation, the awareness which perceives and the form of the perception. Here the indissoluble male and female principles are used to represent the two in oneness, the ineffable ultimate reality.

VERSES 37 - 40

Following the instruction of a Buddha Lama . . .

The path which leads to the experience of the visions described in the last four verses begins with the practice of an examination of mind and the discovery of the Four Characteristics of All Experience. One's teacher should be a man whose accomplishments are manifestly evident. A teacher who leaves doubt as to his ability and attainment is not a suitable vehicle for the faith of the aspirant who is likely to become fearful and unstable at some time during his meditation. A teacher should be generous rather than miserly, patient rather than perfunctory, moral in following the conventions of society rather than a social outcast, energetic rather than indolent and passive. He should observe frequent and regular formal meditation practice and ritual procedure, and he should have the power of awareness which produces an intoxication of compassion. Such a teacher is a master of Dzokchen, the Great Perfection.

The Great Perfection is both the name of a school of meditation and the culmination of the practice of Tantrayoga. It is the highest of the Nyingma disciplines and the most pure of the contemporary lineages of Tantric tradition. The Ris-med renaissance of Khams in eastern Tibet during the middle of last century, led by the gTer-ston 'Jam-dbyangs mKhyen-rtse dbang-po, regenerated the Dzokchen (rdzogs. chen.) tradition. The Western world is fortunate to have the possibility of immediate contact with the Lamas from Khams who left for India in the wake of the invading Chinese in 1959. Atiyoga is the practice of the Great Perfection which is an ultimate consummation or completion. A master of Dzokchen is a Buddha and therefore the best of all teachers.

The mind is withdrawn from the confusion of neurotic preoccupations during the practice of the preceding analytic meditation. Then, when passionate impulse no longer arises and desire for both phenomenal and noumenal has stopped, the antidote to the pain which was the initial stimulant to practice, the discursive analysis and examination of mind, fades away. This is the ground for direct revelation of the Great Perfection. Before Buddhamind can bring continuous and intensive understanding, the exercises of meditation must reject all that obstructs the flow of awareness. Cutting away and purification are the first stages of the path. This direct revelation supplants the long process of moral refinement which is the characteristic of the lower vehicles and brings Dzokchen closer to the Ch'an school of China and the Zen school of Japan.

These verses summarising the development of practice conclude with the image of a bird in the sky. This bird glides through the sky with one wing of skillful means which includes the first five Pāramitās and the other wing of insight which refers to the Prajñāpāramitā, the perfection of discriminating awareness. This bird is the Bodhi-bird known only to the Buddhas and Bodhisattvas.

VERSES 41 - 43

In the teaching of the Noble Tradition . . .

The three careers which stress this mode of meditation are the Śrāvakayāna, Pratyekabuddhayāna and Mahāyāna. Throughout the world of Buddhadharma, now and in the past, this vipaśyanā meditation of examination is the foundation of practice. Methods of presentation differ as do the aims in view, but the essential practice remains the same. Mi-pham Rinpoche has given precise instructions on how to meditate within the total context of the Bodhisattva's development. Both the Śrāvakayāna and the Pratyekabuddhayāna present only a partial view determined by their lesser scope. The Śrāvaka aims at destroying the cause of passionate turmoil and his mundane frustration, ignoring the finer yoga of discovering the nature of Ultimate Reality. The Pratyekabuddha strives to remove both passion and ignorance from his mind but keeps the joy to himself. In the Mahāyāna all practice is developed with the whole of sentient life in mind.

The image of the gold refinery is recurrent in scriptures on meditation to express the subtlety of the process of transforming mind and cultivating it to its highest potential. Meditation must not be forced or, like the greedy monkey who got his fist stuck in the peanut jar trying to extract more than he could well eat, nothing will be gained. But just as the fire which burns the impurities from gold must stay at a constant intensity, so the strength of concentration fixed upon the objects of mind should remain constant during meditation. Pure gold can be molded into whatever form is desired just as mind can be made responsive to the needs of others, taking the shape and producing the vibration necessary to bring harmony.

VERSES 44 - 45

In the Sūtras it is said that . . .

The fourfold truth of the Mahāyāna refers to the same marks of phenomena—compound multiplicity, transcience, the origin of suffering and essential insubstantiality. Although much has been said about the nature of reality beyond a statement of these four characteristics, little of that verbiage adds anything to the truth of the matter. Therefore it is said that the significance of all the topics which have been written down in the Sūtras and explained and learned during the primary stage of learning about the Dharma, rather than experiencing the Dharma, is comparable to the significance of this instruction.

If the significance of this explanation and instruction has been felt then it is imperative that the seed be watered, the young plant tended, and eventually the fruit picked from the mature trees. The quality of the fruit depends on a firm commitment to practice.

Mangalam
May all beings be happy!

Part Two

INSTRUCTIONS ON VISION IN THE MIDDLE WAY

Introduction

A peaceful and clear mind is the point of departure into the rarefied space of compassion which is the ultimate aspiration of the Bodhisattva. This second short text of Lama Mi-pham describes the stages of the path which are passed through towards that end. This is a map to guide and instruct. It begins at the point at which certainty of the absence of a permanent and substantial individuality has arisen and, after passing through the various stages of understanding, ends at the realisation of an indescribable ultimate reality. The process is a paring away of limiting views and reintegration of the mind split between subject and object.

Although an intellectual grasp of this dialectic is an important aid to meditation, it should not be confused with the experiential actuality. This text is as different from the meditation experience as a map is from the terrain which it depicts. This is a finger pointing at the moon rather than the moon itself. However, if no study has been made in a preliminary stage of learning, when during meditation practice these mental states are encountered, great fear may arise and indecision at crossroads will expend valuable energy and time. This short text epitomises the teaching of the masters of the Middle Way synthesised from the experience of generations of practitioners in both India and Tibet. If its ramifications are fully understood then further study is rendered unnecessary.

All practitioners of the Buddhadharma in Tibet are followers of the Middle Way (dbu.ma./Mādhyamika). However, there are two primary schools of discipline which correspond to two different levels of achievement, one developing the meditation experience further than the other. Historically, these schools have been called Prāsaṅgika (thal.'gyur.ba.) and Svātantrika (rang.rgyud.pa.). The subdivisions of these schools are also related to varying degrees of acceptance of the absolute as inexplicable. Within the Svātantrikas some say that ultimate reality is an insubstantial, interdependently related field, while others believe that Emptiness and form are separable experiences. The different lineages of Svātantrika postulate a variety of images and visions to describe ultimate reality, all or any of which may be encountered during meditation. The Prāsaṅgikas, however, reject every attempt at asserting any postulate at all concerning the ultimate experience. The difference of achievement of the practitioners of these schools is well defined in the text. The essential distinction between them is the presence in the former of a profound inherent tendency to rationalise the immediacy of a previous moment in its dross in the present. Here is the pretence that the reflection of the ultimate is different from the ultimate itself. Giving oneself over to the here and now without reservation or hesitation results in a perfect expression of spontaneity in the form which is at hand rather than a prescribed model.

INSTRUCTIONS ON VISION IN THE MIDDLE WAY

Root Verses=Commentary

After examining and purifying mind
Finding the absence of a personal self
And with certainty of this crucial insight
'I' become the composition of the parts.

Examining what is still unknown
Distinguishing between conditioned and unconditioned
Analysing each form of experience
This is called 'this' and that is called 'that'.

Practice of the previous meditation induces certainty that 'I' does not exist in any substantial form. Discovering, however, that what was previously considered to be a concrete entity is a composition of parts which for convenience were categorised under the five groupings of bodymind, the tendency is to identify with the sum of the parts. Continuing meditation by examining whatever arises in the mind, the distinction should be made between the experience of the parts of the bodymind complex and the unconditioned states of concentration which should become more frequent as meditation progresses. Gradually each experience will become well defined, but the object of experience will continue to appear as an independent entity, existing regardless of the other ingredients of the perceptual situation, namely, the organ of sense and the sensation. The habit of belief in the material existence of things is difficult to break. A chair will still be considered as 'existent' even after the perceiver leaves the room.

Still clinging to the various forms of the flow
Searching for substance, nothing is found.
Then going beyond the 'irreducible duality'
(This is explained by science)
Ever finer reductions establishing nothing
An interdependent field appears
Consisting of both the manifestly real
And the fictional fantasies of mind.

So long as there is a belief in the existence of forms independent of the perceiver, the search for the self-existent substance continues. The categories of mind and matter, subject and object, are transcended in this search. But the all-important transformation occurs when all things are seen as an inter-related field evolving in its entirety from one pattern into another. The belief in any 'self' or 'entity' is shattered in this vision of totality. However, the realisation of this higher reality may not be achieved immediately, but more likely, it will first appear as a bright possibility and only with constant perseverance in meditative practice will it become clear. The fictions of mind, the fantasies which have been mistaken for the genuine

102

reality remain to colour the vision in ways that obscure it. These are deeply ingrained habits of perception, insisting that somewhere there is a fundamental distinction between 'I' and 'it', between subject and object, between the poles of every duality.

Focusing whatever must be examined
Both manifest reality and mental fantasy
Closely inspecting with penetrating scrutiny
Neither root nor base is discovered.
So nothing is. But like illusion and dream
Echo, faerie or the moon's reflection in water,
Hallucination or mirage, chimera or phantom,
Meditating on the nature of the apparent Emptiness
        of Illusion—
Emptiness is in form and form in Emptiness.

Continuing to search for the base of existence, everything which enters the mind is scrutinized. Although a vision of reality excluding the limitations of duality and selfishness is dimly perceived, the same process of examination and purification during meditation is essential. Gradually as the vision becomes a constant mode of perception, all things take on an illusory quality, they become lighter and shimmer as if immaterial and gossamer. The realisation dawns that the Emptiness which contains release from the weight of mundane existence is nowhere but in the forms which are perceived. There is nowhere to go to, nothing to discover but the nature of mind.

Such is the specific ultimate reality.
But with the certainty of this realisation
And with an ongoing vision of magical illusion
Understood through unsullied insight
Still bound by the fascination of form
And failing to relax hypnotic ideas
Balked by conceptualisation
The essential pervasive passivity is unseen.

Here the vision is sufficiently developed to perceive the Emptiness in every form and the form in Emptiness, but because of the obscuring function of profoundly rooted habits of thought, the particularising tendency prevents full understanding of the identity of all forms. The intellect still has sufficient power to intensify the discriminating faculty at the expense of the underlying compassion. The details of manifestation still bind attention by means of their decorative quality, and the preconceptions fortified by the common sense assumptions which have previously provided a supporting value system still block pure awareness. In the post-meditative state reality sustains the dreamlike quality which has been developed and insight does not vanish with the completion of formal practice, yet the root causes of delusion remain as subtle and elusive obstacles to full understanding.

When certainty in this magical vision arises
Focus the fascinating vestiges of delusion
And thoughtfully examine them—
No substance to these objects exists.
Then finding no mind which is clinging
Relax, detached in simple freedom
And thus composed, the outer and inner
Stream of images flows unbroken.

The subtle obstacles to the stream of spontaneously apparent forms are removed in the same way as the grossest forms of passion—by means of close attention while searching for the essential nature of the object. The momentarily arising visionary field has some snags in it and pulls mind in that direction, limiting the scope of vision and preventing the full awareness of the breadth and depth of reality. Attention to them, discovering their substantial Emptiness, destroys their fascination. In the same way, attention to the mind which is attracted and which imposes a delusory fiction upon the tapestry of perception discovers no mind. Then having finally destroyed all attachment to both external and internal forms, the distinction between subject and object is destroyed and the all-pervasive ultimate reality is understood. The flow of perception is unimpeded.

In this original state of detachment
All that is woven into the continuum
Primordially unborn and unimpeded
Free from grasping and fascination
Is identified in the realm of self-sameness.
Without assertion of something or nothing
In the flow of ineffable significance
Only unquestionable experience dawns.

With the realisation of the realm of free space in which all things are identified, anything which enters experience is known to be unborn in its origin. This is the attainment of the ultimate refuge, for with complete certainty in the essential reality of whatever is experienced, no fear arises to begin the process of action-reaction producing attraction and aversion, clinging and anxious repulsion and complex reaction patterns. Detached, without any tendency to slow the natural progression from unitary totality to the intimately related flash of the following moment, no doubt or fear arises, no expectancy remains unfulfilled simultaneously with its arising. Rather there is a continuous sense of amazement at the ineffable beauty and sublimity of the being in life and understanding. Nothing need be asserted and nothing need be negated, for the perfection of the moment excludes the possibility of detracting expression which both positive and negative assertions imply. The precise discriminating awareness which is inseparable from the realm of self-sameness prevents the overbalance into an entranced state of blissful unknowing. The

particulars of every situation are perceived, but none bring disquiet for the ultimate relationship between the parts is the harmonising, unifying factor.

The transcendent, all-pervasive ultimate reality is seen
As the suchness of all aspects of experience,
Active self-awareness of distinctions
By passive, undivided understanding.
Meditation is the constant spontaneity
Of coincident Emptiness and relativity,
The two truths become one in the authenticity
Of the Master Adept of the Middle Way.

This is the ultimate reality in which there is no attempt to postulate any formula or metaphor descriptive of the experience of the unity of Emptiness and form. There is no division between thought and experience. Thought has been transformed into the underlying understanding which is inseparable from the self-awareness of the form which is discerned. Like sugar dissolved in water, like heat and fire, or like water and wetness, there is not one without the other. The two truths, the relative empiric truth and the ultimate and absolute truth become one, and the yogin is the knowledge holder in this authentic state of being. This is the culmination of the Mādhyamika Path in what is known to the Tibetans as Umachenpo, the Great Middle.

This nondual immanent understanding
Free of the objectifying process of mind
When desired, can be immediately realised
By following Mantrayāna instruction.
Or this ultimate crucial height
Can be reached after purifying inspection
Attaining gradual conviction on the path
In the Middle Way meditation practice.

The mental state or level of consciousness with which the reader has apprehended the above information and visions is the ground, the starting point. The Nyingma tradition offers two possible vehicles to travel the path to a realisation of the inadequately expressed goal which the visions imply. The first is the direct and immediately efficacious Mantrayāna, and the second the Mādhyamika path of the Mahāyāna which is an easier, slower, and less dangerous means of attaining the same ends.

When a man is parched by thirst
The thought of water brings no relief—
Only drinking can quench his thirst:
So information differs from experience.
The exhausting search for information
For mere objective knowledge
Becomes needless with meditative experience
Which quickly leads to equanimity.

The necessary study which teaches skill in self-expression, metaphysical postulation, logic and other arts and sciences precedes practice. It is customary to look at a map before starting out on a journey. However, to believe that the knowledge which is gained from the map is the terrain itself is to mistake the concept for the reality. No mere intellectual certainty is valuable when faced with the naked reality of the depths of mind. Like accumulated wealth at the moment of death or the gift of snow in the tropics, theoretic knowledge has no relevance out of its own sphere. The spontaneous expression of the view perceived in profound equanimity, which is the acceptance of whatever may arise without addition or subtraction, replaces the preconceptions of dogma and philosophical dicta.

Written by the Great Nyingma master Lama Mi-pham writing under the name 'Jam-dpal dgyes-pa'i rdo-rje on the twenty-ninth day of the eleventh month of the water-dragon year, so that all beings may realise the meaning of the profound Middle Way.

Mangalam
May all beings be happy!

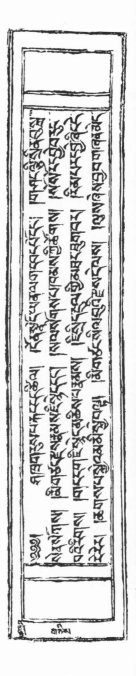

འཇུག་པར་བྱ། །སྟོན་ཆེ་བདག་གིས་དུས་གསུམ་དུ། །རྩལ་མི་ཉན་ཡིད་ལ་འབྱེད་པ་ཡིས། །སྣ་ཚོགས་རྟོག་པ་རྒྱུན་འཇུག་པ། །དེ་ཡི་ཚབ་
ཏུ་འདི་བཞག་བྱ། །ག་ལ་ཏེ་དུབ་པར་གྱུར་ནས་སུ། །གཉེན་པོའི་ཁྱད་པ་ལ་མི་འཇུག་ལ། །ཉོན་མོངས་དགོ་ཀྱང་མི་སྤྱིར། །ཁ་ཏང་
སྒོམ་ས་ཉིད་དུ་ངལ་གསོ་བྱ། །རེ་ཞིག་ངལ་བསོ་ར་རྒྱུད་ནས། །སླར་ཡང་བསྒོམ་བཞིན་སོ་སོར་བརྟག །སོ་སོར་བརྟག་པའི་རྟོགས་པ་
འདི། །དྲན་བཞིན་ཤེས་བཞིན་གསུམ་ཙུ་གནས། །ག་ལ་ཏེ་བཏེང་པར་གྱུར་པའི་སྐབས། །ཉོན་མོངས་སྤྱོ་བར་གྱུར་པ་ན། །དགྲ་བོ་མཐོང་
ཚེ་མཚོན་བཞིན་དུ། །སོ་སོར་བརྟག་པ་བསྣུན་བར་བྱ། །སྐྱུན་པ་ལ་ཐི་ལྷུང་བ་བཞིན། །སོ་སོར་བརྟག་པ་འདི་ལྟར་བྱ། །ཆུང་ངུ་ཉིད་ཀྱིས་ཀྱང

༄༅། ཉོན་མོངས་ལ། །གནོད་པ་ཆེན་པོ་སློས་ཅི་འཚལ། །འདུས་བྱས་ལ་བོར་བའི་ཉེས་པ་རྣམས། །ཅི་ཙམ་མཐོང་བ་དེ་
ཙམ་ལ། །སྐྱོ་ཤེན་འདངས་པ་འདུས་མ་བྱས། །ཞི་བ་སོ་ལ་བླུན་མེད་པ་ཤེས། །གཉིས་པ་རྒྱུད་ལ་སྐྱེས་པའི་ཚད་ནི། ནམ་ཞིག་གོམས་ནས་རང་
གཞན་གྱི། །ཕུང་པོ་ལྔ་དང་འདུས་བྱས་ཀུན། །དུ་མ་ཉིད་དང་དང་མི་རྟག་དང་། །སྡུག་བསྔལ་ཉིད་དང་བདག་མེད་པ། །ངང་གིས་ཐོང་དུ
རྒྱུད་གྲུབ་ནས། །ཆེད་དུ་འབད་པ་མེད་པར་ཡང་། །སྣང་བ་ཐམས་ཅད་ཧ་ལ་རྫོལ་ཏུ། །ཤར་ཚེ་ཉོན་མོངས་མགོ་གནོན་འགྱུར། །ཉོན
མོངས་རླབས་དང་བྲལ་བས་ན། །དེ་ཚེ་རྙོགས་མེད་ཡིད་ཀྱི་མཚོ། །རང་དབང་དགའ་དང་མཐུན་གྱུར་ནས། །ཞི་གནས་ཏིང་ངེ་འཛིན་ལ

ཤེས་རབ་སྙིང་པོའི་ཞལ་གདམས

རིག ། ཕྱག་ཅིག་སེམས་ཀྱི་ངོ་བོ་ཡི། །དེ་ཉིད་བལྟས་ནས་ལྷག་པར་མཐོང་། །འདི་ནི་ཐེག་གསུམ་ཐུན་མོང་གི །དང་པོར་འཇུག
པའི་ལམ་ཡིན་ནོ། །གསུམ་པ་གོ་དོན་ནི། གང་ཆེ་རྟེན་འབྱུང་སྒྱུ་མ་ལྟ་འི། །ཆོས་ཀུན་གཙོ་ནས་མ་སྐྱེས་པས། །ཆོས་བདག་མེད་པའི
སྟོང་ཉིད་ལ། །ཐབ་དང་ཅིག་སོགས་མཐའ་གཉིས་བྲལ། །དབྱེར་མེད་མཉམ་པ་ཉིད་ཀྱི་དབྱིངས། །བདེ་བར་གཤེགས་པའི་སྙིང
པོ་འདི། །དེ་ཉིད་རྟོགས་ནས་གྱི་ངེ་ཞིའི་མཐར། །མི་ཕྱག་ནས་རྒྱུད་བའདས་ཆེན་པོ་འགྲུབ། །དེ་ནི་མཆོག་ཏུ་དགའ་དང་བདེ། །འཕྲུལ་མཁྱུས
ཆེན་པོ་ངེས་སྒྲུབ་རྟག །ཀུན་གཞི་ཆེན་པོའི་ཡེ་ནས་ཁྱེ། །ཕ་རོལ་ཕྱིན་པ་བླ་ན་མེད། །བླ་མེད་ངེས་གསང་སྙིང་པོའི་དོན། །དོན་གྱི

༄༅། །ལྷུན་སྒྲུབ་བདེ་ཆེན་འབྱིངས། །རང་བྱུང་ཡེ་ཤེས་ཉི་ཟླ་ལྟག །རི་ཡི་ངང་ནས་ཆོས་ཀུན་རྫོགས། །དེ་ཉིད་བླ་མའི
མན་ངག་གིས། །ཐང་ཀ་རང་སྒྲོང་རྫོགས་ཆེན་ལུགས། །དེ་ཕྱིར་ཐེག་ཆེན་མདོ་དང་སྔགས། །ཐུན་མོང་ལམ་སྦྱོང་སློབ་འགྲོ་རྒྱུ། །
འདུས་བྱས་འཁྲུལ་པའི་སྣང་བ་ཞིག་ཏུ་ནས། །སོ་སོར་བརྟག་པའི་ལམ་འདི་བཤད། །དང་པོ་སོ་སོར་བརྟག་པའི་མཐུས། །ཉོན
མོངས་སྐྱེ་བའི་མཚན་མ་བཤིག །ཕུང་པོ་སྟོང་པར་ངེས་ཤེས་ནས། །ཁམས་གསུམ་ལ་སྨོན་ཆགས་པ་བྲལ། །དེ་ནས་རིམ་བཞིན
དམིགས་མཚན་ཀུན། །ཉེ་བར་ཞི་བའི་སྟོང་པ་ཉིད། །སྙིང་གཉེན་ཀུན་ལ་མི་སྨོན་པས། །མཐར་རྫིན་ཆགས་པ་ཀུན་བྲལ་འགྱུར། །

INSTRUCTIONS ON VISION
IN THE MIDDLE WAY

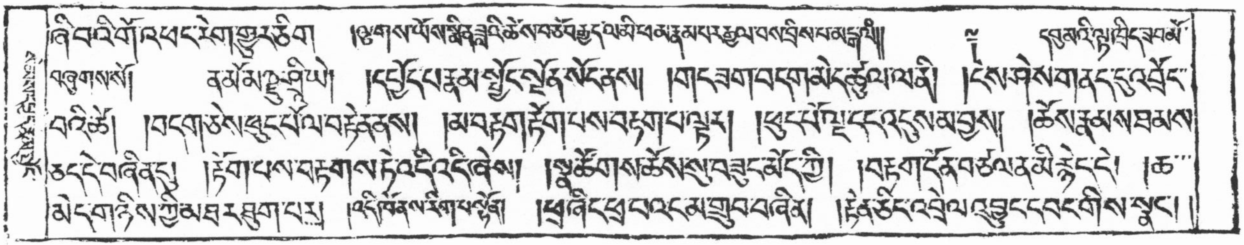

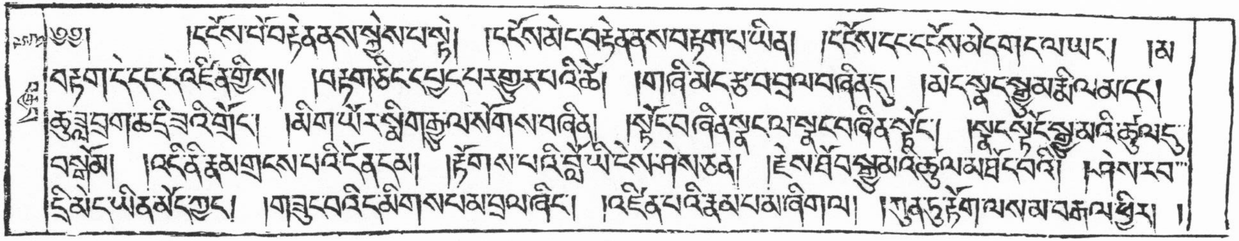

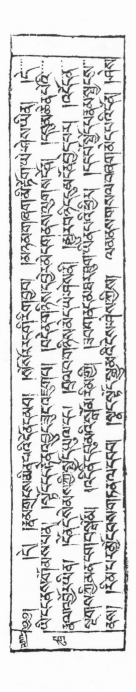

Selected Readings

BUDDHAGHOSA, *The Visuddhi-maggi of Buddhaghosa,* ed. by C.A.F. Rhys-Davids, 2 vols., Pali Text Society by H. Milford, 1920-21

CONZE, EDWARD, *Buddhist Meditation,* Allen and Unwin, 1960

——, *Buddhist Thought in India,* London, Allen and Unwin, 1962

——, *The Prajnaparamita Literature,* Mouton, 'S-Gravenhage, 1960

——, *Vajracchedika Prajnaparamita,* Serié Orientale Roma XIII, 1957

GAMPOPA, *Jewel Ornament of Liberation,* tr. by H.V. Guenther, London, Rider, 1959

GUENTHER,HERBERT V., *Buddhist Philosophy: In Theory and Practice,* Baltimore, Penguin Books, 1971

——, *Philosophy and Psychology in the Abidharma,* Buddha Vihara, Lucknow, 1957

——, *Treasures on the Tibetan Middle Way,* Brill, Leiden, 1970

MURTI, T.R.V., *The Central Philosophy of Buddhism,* Allen and Unwin, London, 1970

RAMANAN, K. VENKATA, *Nagarjuna's Philosophy as Presented in Maha-Prajnaparamita Sutra,* Tuttle, Tokyo, 1966

SANTIDEVA, *The Bodhicaryavatara or Entering the Path of Enlightenment,* MacMillan, London, 1970

STCHERBATSKY, THEODORE, *The Central Conception of Buddhist Nirvana,* Mouton, The Hague, 1965

——, *The Soul Theory of the Buddhists,* Bharatiya Vidya Prakasan, Varanasi, 1970

STRENG, FREDERICK J., *Emptiness — A Study in Religious Meaning,* Abingdon Press, New York and Nashville, 1967

Index

Abhidharma, 36
Anger, 31
Anxiety, 65
Associations, producing positive or negative states of mind, 65
Attachment, 47, 59, 60, 75, 76
Attentiveness, 43
Awareness, 60; discriminating, 25, 33, 106

Bodhisattva, 25, 29 ff., 56, 81-82, 91, 97; vow, 35, 66, 70, 84
Body, 60, 64, 76, 86; analysis of, 15, 16, 43 ff., bodymind, 46, 51, 57, 58, 67, 72, 101
Buddha, 53, 68, 72, 75, 87; Buddhahood, 65, 85; Buddha Lama, 51, 88; Buddha Nature, 68, 87 refuge in, 35 see Dharma
Buddhism, Tibetan, 11 ff., 17; Central Asia, 12; hidden, 17

Compassion, 29, 52, 65, 97
Composure, 65, 80; meditation, sāmatha, 32, 33, 37, 48
'Concealed Teachings', 16, 17
Conditioned nature of existence, 21, 45, 49, 85; Four Marks of Conditioned Existence, 37, 71, 76, 80, 89

Death, 45, 70, 72, 75
Decay, 45, 70, 71, 72
Delusion, 104, 105

Desire, 43, 44, 56, 62, 66, 77, 81; attaining release, 65; destroyed, 51
Detachment, 29, 53, 63, 65, 72, 106
Dharma, 30, 31, 92; Buddhadharma, 34, 35, 78, 90; refuge in, 35
'Discriminating awareness', 33
Dzokchen, the Great Perfection, 89, 90

'Ego', 22; ego-centered, 15; egoistic pride, 56
Emotions, 31, 56 ff., 63, 70, 77, 81
'Empty', 16, 50, 86; empty of self, 47
Emptiness, 32, 47, 51, 52, 53, 67, 75, 82, 88, 98, 103, 104, 105, 108
Energy, 31, 39
Enlightenment, 21, 22; Buddha's, 72
External objects, 61, 62-63, 65, 67, 74

Forcefulness, excessive, in concentration, 41
Forgetfulness, 39-40, 48, 66
Form, 60-61, 66, 88
Friend, 38, 39, 41

Generosity, 25, 30, 87, 89

Habits, 57, 58, 78, 102; destroyed, 78
Hīnayāna, 22, 82

Impermanence, 67, 68, 70, 71
Initiation, 50, 80, 84

INDEX

Insight, 74, 75, 80, 81;
    into composite nature, 37;
    meditation, *vipaśyanā*, 32,
    33, 38, 44, 46, 50, 78, 82
Intellect, 41

Karma, 58, 60, 70

Laziness, 38-39
Lust, 56, 59; *see* Desire

Madhyamika, 98, 108, 109;
    dialectic, 33; texts, 33
Magical illusion, 44, 50, 86,
    104
Mahāyāna, 22, 25, 26, 36, 51,
    53, 82, 85, 91, 92, 109
Manjuśrī, drawing, 24;
    homage, 25
Mantra, 51
Mantrayāna, 109
Meditation, 13 ff., 21, 22, 25, 32
    ff., 67, 71, 76, 80, 81, 82-84,
    89, 91, 97, 98, 101, 108, 109;
    Nine Stages, 82-84; obsta-
    cles in, 38-41; Perfection
    of, 32-33, 87; practice of,
    33-38; practice of dying,
    76; wheel of, 47; Wheel of
    Analytic, root verses, 43-53
Merit, dedicated to others, 36
Middle Way, 41, 97, 108;
    Middle Way Vision, 87
Mind, 62, 63, 64, 66, 67, 71, 72,
    75, 78, 80, 82, 86, 89, 102,
    103, 109; analysis of, 15, 16
Mindfulness, 48, 51, 52, 68, 77,
    78
Mi-pham, 16, 22, 53, 91, 110;
    drawing of, 4
Morality, 25, 30-31, 87, 89

Negative manifestations, 66
'New Tradition', 12
Nirvāna, 55, 78, 87

Numbness of mind, 40-41
Nyingma, 21, 89, 109; *see* 'Old
    Tradition', *rNyingma*

Obstacles, 25, 38-41, 65-66,
    105
'Old Tradition', *rNying-ma*,
    12, 16

Padma Sambhava, 16
Passion, 43, 48, 49, 50, 51,
    55-57, 72, 76, 105;
    six tones of, 56-57
Past lives, 77
Patience, 25, 31, 87
'Peaceful calm', 80, 81;
    calmness, *zhi-gnas*, 38
Perceptions, 63, 64, 66, 68, 74,
    75, 77, 86, 102, 105;
    corrupted, 45
Perfections, the Six, 29 ff., 87,
    90
Perseverance, 25, 31-32, 87,
    102
Practice, 33 ff., 48, 49, 58, 76,
    92, 110
Primordial, 86
Purification, 33, 51, 52, 55, 87,
    101, 103, 109

Reality, 14, 37, 85;
    Ultimate, 86, 88, 91, 97,
    98, 104, 105, 108
Re-birth, 57
Refuge, 35-36, 106
Restlessness, 40-41
Ris-med Renaissance, 89

Samsāra, 81;
    as Nirvāna, 55, 65
Sangha, refuge in, 35
Self, 14, 47, 75, 101, 102; Great
    Self, 51, 87; selfishness, 78;
    selflessness, 53; 'selves', 21
Sense organs, sense fields, 44,

61, 62, 66, 102
Sensory experience, 61;
   data, 64
Sexual desire, 34, 58, 60;
   prowess, 72
Six aspects, or Six Perfections,
   29 ff.
Suffering, 45, 46, 53, 55, 57, 66,
   71, 72, 73, 78; Great
   Transcendence of, 50, 87
Sūtras, 33, 35, 39, 51, 53, 92

Tantras, 51
Tantric tradition, 89
Tibet, early history of
   Buddhism, 11 ff.
Triple Gem, 53, 66

Unborn, 86, 106

Vajrayāna, 22, 82, 85, 88
Vices, the ten, 30
Vipaśyanā, 32, 38, 84, 90-91

Index of Tibetan and Sanskrit Terms
(*Listed according to English alphabet*)

blan.te.'jog.pa., 83
Bodhisattvayāna, 81
dbu.ma., 98
'du.byed., 60
'du.shes., 60
dul.bar.byed.pa., 83
rgyun.du.'jog.pa., 83
bKa'-'gyur, 11
kleśa, 31
lhag-mthong, 38
Mādhyamika, 33, 98
Mya.ngan.'das.chen., 87
rnam.par.zhi.bar.byed.ba., 83
nmyam.par.hjog.par.byed.pa.,
   84
nye.ba.'jog.pa., 83
rNying-ma, 12
nyon.mongs., 31
pañcaskandha, 58
pāramitā, 29, 90
phung.po.lnga., 58
Prāsangika, 98
Pratyekabuddhayāna, 81-82
   90-91
dpyod.pa., 58
rang.rgyud.pa., 98

rūpa, 60
śamatha, 32, 84
samjñā, 60
samjñāskandha, 64, 65
samskāra, 60
śrāvakayāna, 81-82, 90-91
svātantrika, 98
bsTan-'gyur, 11
gter-ma, 16
gTer-ston, 16, 17
thal.'gyur.ba., 98
gtod.pa.'jog.pa., 82
rtog.pa., 58
rtse.gcig.tu.byed.pa., 84
tshor.ba., 60
vedanā, 60
vicāra, 58
vijñāna, 60
vijñānaskandha, 66
vipaśyanā, 32, 33, 38
   44, 46, 53, 78, 82
vitarka, 58
zhi.bar.byed.pa., 83
zhi-gnas, 37, 38
gzugs., 60

(*Note: Silent prefix letters are not alphabetized*)